The INDIANS of NEW JERSEY

by GREGORY EVANS DOWD

TRENTON
NEW JERSEY HISTORICAL COMMISSION, DEPARTMENT OF STATE

Reprint, 2001, Trenton Printing ◀▦▶ ''

New Jersey Historical Commission, Department of State
225 West State Street, P.O. Box 305
Trenton, New Jersey 08625

Designed by Nancy H. Dallaire and Lee R. Parks
Cover designed by Nancy H. Dallaire

Library of Congress Cataloging-In-Publication Data

Dowd, Gregory Evans
  The Indians of New Jersey by Gregory Evans Dowd.
    p. cm.– (New Jersey history series; 3)
  Includes bibliographical references
  ISBN 0-89743-079-4: $9.00
  1. Delaware Indians—History. 2. Indians of North America—New Jersey—
  History. I. Title. II. Series.
  E99.D2D68   1992   92-34212
  974.9'004973—dc20   CIP

TABLE OF CONTENTS

ACKNOWLEDGMENTS

I have received encouragement and helpful criticism in equal measure. Mary Murrin and Lee Parks of the Historical Commission deserve special thanks for their attention to historical content and editorial style at every point. David Cohen, Richard Waldron, and Bernard Bush, also of the Commission staff, read parts of the manuscript and provided many useful suggestions. I have Nancy Dallaire at the Commission to thank for the book's excellent design. Outside the Commission, Lorraine E. Williams of the New Jersey State Museum, Barbara Petrick of Dickinson High School in Jersey City, and Professor Stanley N. Worton of Jersey City State College read early versions of the manuscript and made valuable suggestions on content and accessibility to students.

INTRODUCTION

The first European explorers to encounter Native Americans did not really see them with "the naked eye"; they saw them as they wanted to. The very name that Europeans first called them, "Indians," tells us far more about what the explorers looked *for,* a western passage to Asia, than it does about whom they looked *at.* In time, as the Europeans realized that they were not at the gates of the Far East but at the edge of two "new" continents, they began to call the Native Americans by other names, such as "heathens" and "savages." Like "Indians," these terms reflected ideas the explorers had brought with them more than the actual nature of the American Indians.

When Europeans called Indians "heathens" they meant two things. First, they meant that the people of America were not Christian or Jewish, which was true. Second, they meant that the Indians had no religion, which was false. This pamphlet will show that many of New Jersey's Indians, like other Native Americans, were devoutly attached to complex religious traditions.

By the other term, "savages," Europeans meant that Indians had no society or culture, that they were unpredictable, lawless, and wild. This notion, as this pamphlet will demonstrate, was also false. The people of America, in this case the native people of New Jersey, did not roam freely through a virgin wilderness. They actively managed the woodlands. They cleared fields and cultivated crops. They possessed systems of government, patterns of kinship, and systematic codes of behavior.

Some perceptive Europeans realized that describing the Indians as savage and the Europeans as civilized was unfair. Francis Daniel Pastorius, a German who met New Jersey's Indians in the late 1600s, wrote that calling the Indians savage and the Europeans Christian did "great injustice to many of both varieties." Pastorius thought that Europeans should imitate many of the Indians' virtues. A devout Christian himself, he believed that few European Christians behaved as their religion demanded. He made a practice of calling Native Americans "unsavage savages" and Europeans "nominal Christians."[1]

But before going too far into the shortcomings of the Europeans' approach to the Native Americans, we should ourselves attempt to view the Indians of New Jersey with our "naked eyes." It is a difficult task. One method of shedding our modern preconceptions is to ask what the Indians themselves thought of their world and of the changes wrought by European colonization. To get at this complicated issue, this pamphlet will raise four essential questions:

1. What were some important differences between the Indians' ideas about the world and the Europeans' ideas?

2. What did the Indians first think of the strangers from the east, and how did their experience with the newcomers change that thinking?

3. How did the European presence change the Indians' world? How did it change their world view?

4. What sort of identity have the descendants of the precolonial New Jersey Indians maintained, both within the state and in other places?

This pamphlet asks its readers to forget much of what they have learned about Indians, to forget the screaming warbonnets of the Hollywood Westerns and the proud but sad and silent Indians of the antipollution campaigns. It asks its reader to forget such words as "primitive" and "civilized." It invites its reader to step into a world that was different, to see how that world fell apart, and to understand why that world's people did what they did to survive.

CHAPTER ONE

Lenapehoking:
The Indians' New Jersey

Most of the vast history of American Indians eludes us. It always will. Some say this is because the Indians left no writings. But the Indians possessed and still possess a rich body of spoken traditions. Why do these fail to reveal their history? One answer is that today's historians think of history differently than the traditional custodians of Indian myth do. The experiences of Native Americans in their thousands of years on the American continents differed profoundly from the history of the Europeans, whose tradition governs today's historical writing. Those of us with modern educations tend to think of history as something that builds over time; western historians sometimes represent history in time lines. For Indians, time was not linear, but cyclical. Indian legends thus have a shape that is difficult for Americans with modern educations to comprehend.

To understand that the Native Americans of history saw things in their own way is to understand the most fundamental of things about them: they had their own ways of seeing, their own ways of doing things. They developed these ways over the thousands of years during which they discovered, settled, and cultivated North America.

This chapter explores the history of the people of a land that the foremost New Jersey anthropologist, Herbert C. Kraft, calls *Lenapehoking*. *Lenapehoking* is an Indian place name for the land that stretched from eastern Pennsylvania and northern Delaware to southeastern New York and western Long Island. It centered on the region between the Delaware River and the Atlantic Ocean—the land we now call New Jersey. First the chapter employs a modern, linear approach to trace the history of the Indians in Lenapehoking. Then it examines three of the many cyclical patterns in Indian culture—peace and war, summer and winter, birth and death—that gave rich meaning to the Native American view of history.

Discovery, Settlement, and Cultivation

At least thirteen thousand years ago, in the midst of an ice age, the wide plain that now rests at the bottom of the shallow Bering Sea between Siberia and Alaska became the footpath of the human discoverers of America. We will never know why the Paleo-Indians, ancestors of the American Indians, walked across the thousand-mile-wide path from Asia, but archaeologists generally assume that the hunters and their families were after big game.

For thousands of years the Paleo-Indian hunters pursued mammoths, mastodons, musk oxen and caribou as they skirted the glaciers and fanned out across the continents. By about 12,500 years ago, groups of them were hunting in what is now New Jersey.

The Paleo-Indians, according to Kraft, "demonstrated a superb mastery of flint technology."[1] With only stone, bone, and wood at their disposal, they fashioned drills, scrapers, pins, and graceful "fluted" spearheads. They carefully selected the stones to be used in crafting their tools, sometimes traveling or trading over hundreds of miles to obtain the best materials. Although we know little of their daily lives, we assume that, like other hunting-and-gathering peoples, they divided labor between men and women: the men hunted and fished while the women gathered edible and medicinal plants.

For unknown reasons, the mammoths and mastodons died off in North America within a few thousand years of the Paleo-Indians' entry into Lenapehoking. Hunters now had to rely on middle-sized game such as white-tailed deer, black bear, and elk, as well as smaller mammals, turkey and other birds, and fish. But if the loss of big game challenged the Indians, they gained a rich plant environment around seven thousand years ago, when nut-producing deciduous trees replaced the subarctic evergreens, providing forage for both animals and people. Some five thousand years ago Indian men began using fishing nets, fish traps called weirs, and spearthrowers or *atlatls*. Women employed milling stones, mortars and pestles to grind seeds, nuts, berries, and dried fish into meals that could be stored for hungry times. Between three thousand and two thousand years ago, New Jersey's Indians learned the art of making cookware, first of stone and later of clay. About one thousand years ago they planted their first gardens, growing the "three sisters" of Native American agriculture: corn, beans, and squash.

By seven hundred years ago Indian life had taken a shape that the New Jersey Indians of the colonial period would have recognized. Bows and arrows had replaced the atlatl and the spear; large clay cooking pots furnished most households; dugout canoes plied the waters; corn, beans, squash, and meat kept the Indians well fed.

The Lenapes and their Languages

Small villages, each one under its own political rule, dotted the rivers and streams of *Lenapehoking*. The people of the region spoke two related Algonquian languages. North of the Raritan River and the Delaware Water Gap they spoke Munsee, and south of these natural boundaries they spoke Unami. Each village acted independently of all others, though neighboring villages frequently shared the bonds of family and friendship. During the late seventeenth and early eighteenth centuries, after the Munsees and Unamis had begun migrating west, they began to associate with each other. The English began to apply their name for the Unamis, the *Delawares*, to the Munsees as well, and eventually the Munsees themselves accepted the term. The Unamis called themselves the *Lenapes* ("the people"). This pamphlet will follow their eighteenth-century habit, calling both the Munsees and the Unamis the Lenapes. But it should be remembered that while these groups lived in New Jersey they did not form a single Indian nation—or even two nations, for villages remained the essential political units.

The size of the Lenape population before the coming of Europeans is impossible to establish. The usual estimates range from eight to twelve thousand, but these are little better than educated guesses drawn from bad evidence.

However many Lenapes there were, however strong their language differences or independent their villages, they shared

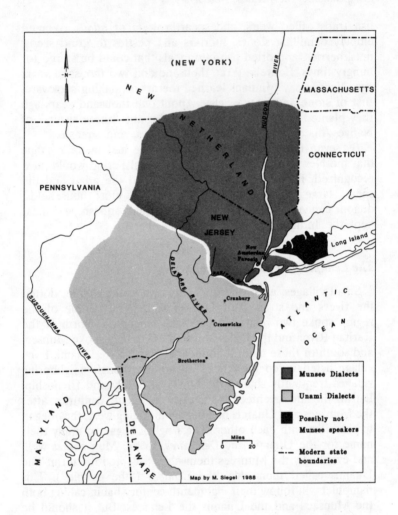

Languages and Locations. *The shaded areas indicate the probable range of the Unami and Munsee dialects when the Dutch arrived. The map also shows important locations mentioned throughout the book, but note that these locations were significant in different periods.* MAP BY MICHAEL SIEGEL; INFORMATION FROM IVES GODDARD, "DELAWARE," AND "EASTERN ALGONQUIAN LANGUAGES," IN HANDBOOK OF THE NORTH AMERICAN IN-DIANS VOL. 15, NORTHEAST, ED. BRUCE TRIGGER (WASHINGTON, DC, 1978), 213–39, 70–77.

much in common. The Netherlander, John de Laet, put it well in 1625 when he wrote that the Indians, "being divided into many nations and people, differ much from one another in language though very little in manners."[2] It is to their shared customs, and the thought that lay behind them, that this chapter now turns.

Government in Peace and War

If we can trust sources from the eighteenth and nineteenth centuries, each of the autonomous (self-governing) Lenape villages was governed by at least two chiefs, a council, and the people at large. One of the chiefs, the sachem, held authority only in peacetime, and even then his authority was limited. One nineteenth-century Lenape wrote of the peace chiefs, "they govern more by persuasion than by coercion, [and] whenever their acts give general dissatisfaction their power ceases."[3] The office was partly hereditary, partly elective. The council, or the village at large (it varied from place to place), selected the leader, but he had to be from the right family.

When an important decision had to be made, the peace chief and the council gathered at the chief's house, and after as much discussion as the people deemed necessary the council members shouted their assent or disapproval of measures, deciding the matter. The peace chief advised the council, mediated in village disputes, and directed such village operations as communal hunting drives or the tracking down of murderers. He also played a religious role, naming the time for the major ceremonies.

The peace chief was no richer than his neighbors. In fact he might sometimes be poorer, for he maintained his popularity in part by distributing presents to the people, saving only a small portion for himself. In this he practiced good Indian economics: goods were not to be hoarded to oneself but distributed to improve one's relations with others. In general, property was not owned by the individual, but by the family or the village as a whole. The Quaker William Penn wrote that among the Lenapes "Wealth circulates like the blood, all parts partake."[4]

When the village was at war, the limited authority of the peace chief almost disappeared, and war chiefs took over. The office of war chief, as the Netherlander Adriaen Van der Donck noted in the seventeenth century, was based on merit, not heredity. Any particularly successful warrior who could gather a sizeable party of followers became a war chief and remained one as long as he was a successful leader. With a war's end, the peace chief resumed his limited authority.

This system of government, characterized by a great deal of personal liberty, yet also a great equality of wealth, remained mostly intact throughout the early years of European contact.

The Annual Round

One of the reasons for the limited authority of the peace chiefs may have been that their villages, though essentially permanent, were unoccupied during much of the year. For fall and winter the villagers divided into small groups and dispersed to various locations for hunting and fishing, where they were beyond the influence of any single village authority. The systematic pattern of gathering and dispersal fits in with what anthropologists call a "seasonal round" or a "subsistence cycle."

As spring approached, the women and some of the men gathered at the village. Together, they prepared the fields for planting, sometimes setting fire to the fields to clear away brush. In the late spring, the men who had continued hunting and fishing joined them. During the summer, the season of great ceremonies, the women worked the crops while the men fished in the rivers and hunted small game. After the harvest, women dried the crops and stored them in pits while the men carefully burned the woods to clear out the underbrush. According to Van der Donck,

The bush burning presents a grand and sublime appearance. . . . Notwithstanding the apparent danger of the entire destruction of the woodlands by the burning, still the green trees do not suffer. The outside bark is scorched three or four feet high, which does them no injury, for the trees are not killed.[5]

Such burning provided better forage for the deer and easier tracking for the hunter. The Indians also frequently employed fire in the communal deer drives of autumn.

As winter approached, the villagers packed up their gear and went to their dispersed hunting territories. At midwinter, the

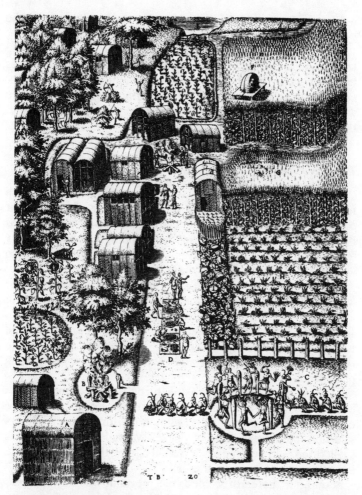

John White, The Town of Secota. *This town in maritime North Carolina resembles the towns of the Lenape in certain respects. It differs in that Lenape houses were likely to have had rounded ends and to be covered with bark rather than with mats. In addition, religious fixtures such as the circle of carved posts and the "Tombe" at the bottom of the painting have no direct parallels among the Lenapes. Nonetheless, in showing regular settlement, somewhat casual eating patterns, and the importance of corn and the forest, the painting has much to say about the lives of most of the peoples of eastern North America.* COURTESY WILLIAM L. CLEMENTS LIBRARY, THE UNIVERSITY OF MICHIGAN AT ANN ARBOR.

women and some of the men returned to the village, and the
cycle resumed.

The cycle that turned from the summertime village to the
wintertime camp met not only the material needs of the Lenapes
but also their human desire for spiritual fulfillment and for
entertainment. Summer was the ceremonial season, and in the
winter visitors to camp could keep a family up all night around
the fire, recounting long stories.

The Creation

Among the many myths of the Lenapes were some which
reveal their way of looking at the world, their vision of their
own history, and their idea of nature. One of these myths has
been recorded in various forms from the seventeenth century
to the present; it is found not only among the Lenapes but also
among other Algonquian Indians and the Iroquois.

The first human being, the story goes, fell from heaven. She
was a pregnant woman; her husband had cast her off. For a
long time she fell without any hope of finding safety. The
Iroquois of New York say that the birds caught her and carried
her for a while. Finally, according to the Lenapes, a sea turtle
rose from the ocean deeps and offered the woman a resting
place upon her shell.

Land formed gradually on the turtle's back. Some Indians
believed that a swimming creature dived to the bottom of the
ocean and brought up earth to pile on the turtle's back. Others
said that the floating scum of the sea washed up on the turtle's
shell, dried, and became land. But all agreed that the earth rode
a turtle swimming upon the seas.

Soon after the earth formed, the pregnant woman went into
labor. At first she bore three "children": a deer, a bear, and
a wolf. Then she continued to bear creatures until she had filled
the world with living things, including twin boys "from whom
the inhabitants of this land are descended."[6]

Since that time, one version of the myth says,

all mankind, wherever they be, are always born with the nature
of one or the other of the aforesaid animals. They are timid
and innocent like the deer; they are brave, revengeful, and just
of hand, like the bear; or they are deceitful and bloodthirsty,
like the wolves.[7]

The myth conveys clearly the Lenapes' close identification with nature: Animals rescue the mother of mankind, and she in turn becomes the mother of many in the animal kindgom. The Lenapes believed that humans, animals and many plants all had spirit lives. John Heckewelder, a missionary who spent many years with the Lenapes, wrote, "They do not exclude other animals from their world of spirits, the place to which they expect to go after death."[8] The Lenapes emphasized this view of their relationship with nature in many of the ceremonies and rituals that marked their progress through the various cycles— war and peace, the annual round, and, as we shall see, life.

Lenape Childhood

The Indians' love for their children impressed visiting Europeans. Roger Williams, writing of the Lenapes' New England neighbors, the Narragansetts, noted that: "Their affections, especially to their children, are very strong."[9] An eighteenth-century missionary observed that Lenape children were not punished but only reproached with words.

Lenape mothers protected their infants with cradleboards. "They lay them on a straight, thin board, little more than the length and breadth of the child, and swaddle it fast upon the board to make it straight."[10] Some writers have suggested that the primary purpose of the cradleboard was to flatten the back of a child's head, but other indications are that it was intended both to protect the infant and to permit the mother to work in the fields with her baby on her back or resting safely nearby. As soon as a child could walk, the cradleboard was abandoned, and the child was free to explore the village under the scrutiny of elders.

The Lenape family structure differed from the typical modern American one. Descent was *matrilineal;* that is, Lenapes determined their descent from the mother's side only. The central branch of a child's family consisted of his siblings (sisters and brothers), his mother and her siblings, her mother and her siblings, and so on.

Lenapes were also *matrilocal:* the family lived in the mother's village. Though the father usually lived in the same house as his wife and children, he did not own it. The house and almost everything in it belonged to the mother and her relatives. The father, though a husband, was something of a permanent guest.

Both points are important for an understanding of a child's relationship with his or her father. The father usually lived at the child's home and had a special relationship with his children, but he did not belong to the same *lineage*. The mother's brother, who did belong to the lineage, often played a very important role in the family, much more important than the role of most American uncles today.

Young Lenape children went naked during the summer. As they grew older the girls wore knee-length skirts of dressed deerskin or woven hemp. Boys wore dressed deerskin breechcloths, "which they gird around their waists, and draw up a fold to cover their nakedness, with a flap of each end hanging down in front and rear." During the winter all the people wore skin, fur, and feather cloaks. Women wore their long hair in braids, either hanging down their backs or tied up in buns. Men plucked or shaved most of the hair off their heads, keeping only a tuft, which they grew into a long braid and decorated with feathers. Both men and women anointed their hair with bear fat so liberally "that it shines so that one can see one's reflection in it." Both also wore paint, tattoos, and earrings, and cut and stretched their earlobes into large, fleshy rings.[11]

Women and Agriculture

The Lenapes marked a girl's entry into womanhood at her first menstruation. Menstruation held powerful meaning for the Lenapes, as it did for most North American Indians. It identified women with powerful life forces that could be dangerous to men.

At the onset of her first period, a girl went off to a separate house. She was not necessarily alone; other women might practice their menstrual seclusion with her, and she could be visited by nonmenstruating women. They brought her food, which she ate with a stick, for it was considered unhealthy to touch food during the period. She cut her hair short and avoided touching it. If her head itched she scratched it with a stick. The girl remained in the hut until the end of her second period, when she washed, dressed in her finest clothes, adorned herself with beads, and put on the partial veil that announced her eligibility for marriage.

Young women frequently took the initiative in seeking a husband. One seventeenth-century observer noted that "men seldom make the first overtures, unless success is certain."[12] Many marriages were arranged by parents, but usually with the consent of the involved couples. Once she had married, a Lenape woman would in all probability be her husband's only wife, for polygamy, though it occurred, was rare. Lenape women never had more than one living husband.

The young couple lived with the woman's family until it decided to furnish a household of its own. The woman made most of the household items. She wove mats of grasses, which were used for bedding, furnishings, and even waterproof walls. She spun rope, not only for cordage but also for rope bags, baskets, and nets. Most important, perhaps, she shaped and fired clay pottery, usually in the form of large beehive or spherical pots without legs, which she set in the fire for cooking. She also fired clay tobacco pipes for both herself and her husband. The woman owned all of these things, as she owned the food she prepared.

One of the most significant contributions of women to Lenape life was the cultivation of corn. As the Lenape staff of life, corn was sometimes eaten on the cob but was more often eaten in the form of cornmeal, cornbread, corncakes, parched cornflakes, and as a base in soups. The woman pounded the corn into flour with a stone or wooden pestle in a large, wooden mortar which had been carved and burned from the trunk of a tree. She sifted the flour in a grass basket and prepared it to her liking, often with beans, berries, squash, fish or meat.

Many varieties of corn were raised. Women planted the seeds in small mounds, far enough apart to allow space for walking. When the corn grew a few inches high, they added beans to the mounds. As the beans grew they used the living cornstalks as beanpoles and also prolonged the fertility of the soil, since beans are nitrogen-fixing plants. Women worked the fields with the assistance of girls and old men, while boys practiced the bow and arrow, protecting the fields from pests.

At only one task did the men contribute significantly to crop production: they helped clear the fields. They cut through the

bark of the trees to kill them, burned them after they had dried, and then cleared them away. After that, the men stayed out of the fields, which became the women's domain.

In the Lenape view, powerful spirit forces also assisted the women in the fields. These forces had to be honored in ceremony. With the first harvest came the Green Corn Ceremony, a major annual celebration that probably formed the basis of the Big House Ceremony that the Lenapes have celebrated in modern times. One form or another of the ceremony was practiced by most of the agricultural Indians of eastern North America from New England to the Gulf of Mexico. During the Green Corn Ceremony, which could last twelve days, the Lenapes thanked the spirit, the Corn Woman, for the crop she had given them. We met this spirit earlier as the first human being. Her existence demonstrates the depth of the Lenape identification of women with agriculture.

After a girl's coming of age, she began a life centered around the household, the village and the fields. Her life focused on those regions of the world over which the Lenapes had the most control. She inhabited the realm of culture: the realm in which friendly human beings shared power with nature in a fairly predictable equilibrium. This equilibrium could be upset by drought, famine, or pestilence; to counteract these dangers the Indians practiced the Green Corn Ceremony, which had been taught them, they said, by the Corn Woman.

Guarding the Corn Fields, Seth Eastman. This nineteenth-century drawing represents Sioux or Chippewa Indians near the headwaters of the Mississippi River, not the Lenapes of New Jersey. The absence of trees and the appearance of a Tepee (a type of dwelling New Jersey's Indians did not use) give this away. But if this drawing, by an army officer who knew the Indians well, is compared with John White's drawing of the Town of Secota, the wide distribution of similar agricultural practices among Indians of much of North America becomes apparent. Note the raised platforms above the cornfield. Note also that it is women who tend these fields, just as it was in Lenapehoking. SOURCE: HENRY ROWE SCHOOLCRAFT, HISTORY, CONDITIONS AND PROSPECTS OF THE INDIAN TRIBES OF THE UNITED STATES *(PHILADELPHIA, 1853), VOL. 3, PLATE 5.*

Men and Animals

The boy's coming of age placed him in a different world, a world apart from the cornfields and even, to some degree, apart from the household. His "vision quest" marked his arrival at adulthood.

As a boy approached manhood, parents and related elders suddenly and systematically pretended to treat him badly. The boy was probably prepared for this. The adults pretended, in the words of one anthropologist, "to drive the child forth from the shelter of home to become a friendless wanderer." The family put on the show "to deceive some spirit force into taking the victim under its protection."[13]

Thus began the Lenape vision quest. Leaving home, hungry and alone, the boy took to the woods, found a suitable spot, prayed for help, made offerings and slept. If he was lucky, a vision came, and he received his protector, his "guardian spirit." Early in the twentieth century a Lenape told an anthropologist about how he had obtained his guardian spirit:

> When I was a boy, I was once fast asleep on a hill near a little creek. Someone said, "Wake up. Let us go to where our friends are!" So I got up and followed him across the little creek and up a hill, where I saw six men sitting on a log.... After they had shaken hands with me they all danced around in a ring.... A little farther on they said: "We will now leave you. Watch us as we go." They went to the east a little way, and then I saw them trotting. They were wolves, and I had thought all the while that they were human beings.[14]

This Lenape had received the wolf as his guardian spirit. From that time on, he would make offerings to the spirit of the wolf, seeking its aid in all his trials. According to Peter Lindestrom, a Swede who lived on the Delaware River with the Lenapes during the seventeenth century, the Indian hunter fashioned a symbol of his spirit and carried it in a pouch on his body. He had such faith in the guardian, Lindestrom wrote, "that the night he dreams about him, he will at once the following day be able to shoot as much game and catch as much fish as ever he wants to."[15]

The vision quest for a guardian spirit, unlike a girl's menstrual separation, did not signify a boy's readiness for marriage. But

Costume of Misinghali 'kun. *This mask and costume were worn in nineteenth-century Big House Ceremonies after the Lenapes had left New Jersey. They may well resemble the New Jersey Lenapes' ceremonial representations of the Mesingw or Living Solid Face, the spirit most important to Lenape hunters.* COURTESY OF MUSEUM OF THE AMERICAN INDIAN, HEYE FOUNDATION, NEW YORK.

for boys who received guardian spirits, the vision quest was a major milestone. It gave them access to the spirit world, a world of sacred power. Lenape hunters, fishermen, and warriors eagerly sought that access.

While women worked the fields and their crops, men worked the forest. There they hunted, fished, and gathered building materials for the village. Through the forests they traveled to trade or fight with other villages. The forest was their special domain, but they did not rule it. In their eyes, they merely worked it in cooperation with its many spirit forces.

From the woods near the village men gathered hickory saplings and chestnut bark to construct homes for their families. They bent the saplings to form frames and covered the frames with large sections of bark. Two types of houses bordered the streams along which the Lenapes lived. The longhouse, similar to the home of the Lenapes' Iroquois neighbors, could reach a length of sixty feet. Built in the shape of a quonset hut but with rounded ends, a longhouse usually sheltered several nuclear families from a single lineage. The longhouse belonging to the chief's lineage sometimes doubled as a ceremonial center. Another type of house, the smaller, circular wigwam, may also have been used. A single nuclear family, consisting of mother, father and children, dwelled within each one. Wigwams were probably more common at the winter hunting camp than at the summer village.

Lenape house builders could not use logs or planks because their stone implements could not conveniently cut thick wood. The principal use of their stone knives and hatchets in carpentry was to strip bark, cut saplings, or smooth over rough spots. So when they needed to fell large trees, as they did to make both their dugout canoes and their corn mortars, they used fire. The practice was described in the eighteenth century by a traveling German: "They set fire to a great quantity of wood at the roots of the tree, and make it fall by that means." To keep the fire from spreading up the trunk, they blocked it with clay or wet skins. To hollow out the inside of a dugout canoe, the informant went on, "they lay dry branches all along the felled trunk of the tree as far as it must be hollowed out. They then put fire to those branches, and as soon as they are burnt, they are replaced by others."[16] After the canoe was sufficiently hollowed, they scraped it out and shaped it with stone hatchets, knives and planes. Dugouts thirty and forty feet long were common.

Lenapes may also have made bark canoes, but the materials for making them were not often found in Lenapehoking. Dugouts were certainly more typical. They not only provided transportation but also served as an important tool for fishing. "They live in summer mostly on fish," a seventeenth-century observer reported.[17] Lenapes probably took in their catch with dragnets, spears, weirs, hooks and lines, and bows and arrows. Women prepared fresh fish throughout the summer and preserved both dried fish meal and smoked shellfish for winter chowders.

Men hunted deer, bear, beaver, turkey, and smaller game the year round, but autumn was the principal season for deer, and winter for bear. When they hunted alone, they used tall bows strung with braided sinew and long arrows tipped with stone arrowheads. When hunting in groups, as in the autumnal deer hunt, they often used fire to drive a herd toward waiting bowmen. Most bears, according to Van der Donck, were "taken during their sleeping season, when they are most easily killed."[18] The hunters approached the lairs of the hibernating bears and smoked the drowsy beasts into the open.

Although hunting required many technical skills and good knowledge of the habits of the prey, Indian hunters did not believe that skill and knowledge alone could make a successful hunter. Hunters did not, as far as the Lenapes and their Indian neighbors were concerned, surprise and kill beasts. Rather, they invoked rituals which, as Henry Rowe Schoolcraft† wrote, were "supposed to operate in such a manner on the animal sought for, that he voluntarily enter[ed] the hunters' path."[19]

Indians believed that a spirit presided over each species of animal. Such spirits were often the ones that came to boys in their vision quests. In the Lenape language, these beings were *manitowuk*, which was plural for *manito*. *Manito* appears to have meant "spirit force," or "sacred power." The term probably referred both to the spirit and to the spirit's powers.

In the autumn, when the deer looked fat with the summer's good eating, and as their hides grew thick for the coming winter, Lenape villagers attempted to get on good terms with the

---

†For all terms so marked, see appendix, pp. 81-84.

manitowuk of the animals. If the spirits listened to the hunters' prayers they made beasts present themselves to be killed.

Once a hunter had killed a beast, he celebrated another series of observances. John M'Collough, an adopted captive of the Lenapes, observed an elaborate hunting ceremony:

> When the hunting season commences, the first large buck they kill, they cut the neck off the body, close to the shoulders, carry it home with the horns on; they kindle a large fire, placing wood east and west; lay the offering in the middle of the fire, with the face of it towards the east; they take the tarapin shell, with a parcel of small white stones in it, and walk around the fire, rattling the shell, and singing very loud, until the whole is consumed. The rest of the family sitting round the fire the whole time without uttering one word; neither will they eat of any of the flesh of the buck, til after the offering is entirely consumed.[20]

Lenape hunters performed such ceremonies both to "ask the pardon" of the *manitowuk* and to insure like success in the future, for "although it is an authorized and lawful prey, there is something like an accountability, not to God, but to the animal's soul." Hunters, then, did not just take aim and fire. As Frank Speck† has written, for American Indians, hunting was "a holy occupation."[21]

Death and Afterlife

It is not possible to draw a firm line between Lenape religion and other aspects of Lenape life. When women knew their crops were ready for the first harvest, they participated in rituals

John White, Indians fishing. Although the Indians portrayed in this painting are from the Roanoke region of North Carolina in the 1580s, it is likely that the techniques shown were also employed by New Jersey's coastal Indians. Note the spears, the weir, and the dugout canoe. Note also the use of fire for night fishing. John White, the painter, intended this painting as a composite showing various North American plants, animals, people, and fishing techniques to his English countrymen. He did not intend it as a representation of everyday Indian life. COURTESY BRITISH MUSEUM.

honoring the spirits who governed their fields of corn. When men prepared for the hunt, they tried to get on good terms with their prey's *manito*. From the birth of a child to the coming of adulthood, and even to death and the grave, religious ritual pervaded all.

The Lenapes buried the bodies of their dead with goods that were "necessary for the journey to the other world. Then they placed as much wood around the body as will keep the earth from it." Stones and wood, placed on top of the grave, protected it from scavengers, and the relatives of the deceased preserved the site "with religious veneration and care."[22]

Mourning the dead, close relatives painted themselves black; some wore the paint for a full year. Lenapes also refused to mention the name of a dead relative or neighbor and reproached anyone who did so: "the name of the deceased is never mentioned in the presence of the relations; or when the name is mentioned, it is received as if designed to produce mortification, and as an act of unkindness."[23]

Lenapes held, according to the eighteenth-century missionary David Brainerd, that twelve days after dying,

> Departed souls all went *southward*, and that the difference be-
> tween the good and the bad was this: that the *former* were
> admitted to a beautiful town with *spiritual* walls, and that the
> latter would forever hover around these walls in vain attempts
> to get in.[24]

New Jersey's Lenapes, it seems, did not believe that evil persons would go to a fiery hell, but that they would be excluded from the company of loved ones in the next life.

The Supreme Being and Other Manitowuk

Lenapes believed in something like a heaven, but they did not believe in hell. Similarly, they worshiped a Supreme Being, a Creator, a Great Spirit, but they did not believe in a ruling satanic spirit. "Besides the Supreme Being," wrote a missionary in the eighteenth century, "they believe in good and evil spirits, considering them as subordinate deities. . . . They seem to have . . . no idea of the *Devil*, as the Prince of Darkness."[25]

The Creator, the Lenapes told Van der Donck, "is good, kind, and compassionate ... [and] will not punish or do any injury to any person." Unlike the God of Christians, Jews and Muslims, the Lenapes' Great Spirit was remote. He "therefore [took] no concern himself in the common affairs of the world, nor [did] he meddle with the same."[26] Instead, he created the *manitowuk* to manage affairs for him.

The sun, one of these powerful *manitowuk,* watched the earth for the Creator. A male spirit, the sun wore the "finest of deerskin garments, with his face handsomely painted, and wearing red feathers in his hair." He crossed the sky by day and returned beneath the earth at night. When Lenapes took oaths "they [swore] by the sun, which ... [saw] all things."[27]

The moon, a female spirit, watched the earth at night. Like a Lenape woman, she had "great influence over vegetation." Perhaps she was a manifestation of the Corn Goddess, who abided "in the far heavenly region in the image of an aged woman, with dominion over all vegetation."[28] A very different kind of *manito* guarded the animals. According to the anthropologist Mark Harrington, he was called the "Living Solid Face."† He lived in a distant mountain range, but entered the forest now and then to herd deer. He was ritually manifested among the Lenapes by a large red-and-black wooden mask, a body suit of bearskin, and a turtle-shell rattle. The mask had to be offered tobacco now and then. For a safe and successful hunt Lenapes maintained good spiritual relations with the Living Solid Face, as well as with the *manitowuk* of the animals.

Two other kinds of *manitowuk* deserve special mention: the Thunderers and the Great Horned Serpents. Found in myths throughout Native North America, the Thunderers were huge, benevolent, winged *manitowuk* that protected the people from the dangerous, malevolent Great Horned Serpents. The Serpents, or water monsters, were among the few truly evil beings in the Lenape universe. They represented the chaotic world below, while the Thunderers represented the heavenly world above. During thunderstorms, it was said, Thunderers and Serpents clashed.

Conclusion

The Lenapes of *Lenapehoking,* heirs to many thousands of years of history and tradition, saw the world differently than the Europeans of the sixteenth and seventeenth centuries did. Lenapes generally held hospitality in higher regard than wealth; with Europeans it was usually the reverse. Lenape speakers avoided argument; Europeans esteemed verbal aggressiveness. Lenape women were the principal food producers and property holders in *Lenapehoking,* while in Europe men tilled the soil and owned most of the property. The Lenapes sought a close spiritual connection with the powers of nature; the Europeans sought to gain control over nature in order to extract its wealth. Finally, history moved in circles in *Lenapehoking.* Power shifted between peace chiefs and war chiefs. Women and men followed a life cycle of birth, puberty, marriage, death, and rebirth in the afterworld. Ceremonies insured the continuance of the seasons and kept the cycles in motion.

But the Lenapes' ceremonies have all but stopped, and few Lenapes remain in old *Lenapehoking.*

CHAPTER TWO

Contact to 1664: Trade, War and Disease

New People in an Old World

In the spring of the year called by European Christians 1524, Lenape fishermen and shore-dwelling women looked out across the water from the Navesink Highlands and Staten Island to see their first sailing vessel. Contrary to popular myth, they were neither afraid nor confused. They were overjoyed. The record is clear on this. The ship's commander later remembered that as the French and Italian sailors guided their ship toward the Verrazano Narrows, the Indians "came toward us joyfully, uttering loud cries of wonderment, and showing us the safest place to beach the boat." While the Europeans sailed into the upper bay, the Indians in "their small boats ran to and fro across the lake [the bay] with innumerable people aboard who were crossing from one side to the other to see us."[1] But heavy winds arose, preventing Giovanni de Verrazano† from meeting the Lenapes and in fact forcing him out to sea. The Lenapes may have been disappointed. They could not know that Verrazano's ill wind blew them good, and delayed, for many years, a devastating rush of new diseases into *Lenapehoking*.

Just when the next European visited the Lenapes is a matter of conjecture. Until Henry Hudson† made his voyage in 1609, no direct record of a visit survives, but such visits probably took place. To the north, European fishermen frequented the American coast between Maine and Labrador from 1504 on. In a single day in 1542, over sixty ships left the French port of Rouen

31

to fish off Newfoundland, and in 1578, three hundred European ships cruised the same waters. To the south, the Spanish explored Cape Fear, North Carolina, in 1526 and established a Jesuit mission in the Chesapeake region in 1570. The Lenapes, living between these two areas of European contact, may have heard of the Europeans from other Indians, or they may have met the newcomers directly. But the story, as we have a record of it, does not really begin until either 1598, when some accounts say Dutch traders began to frequent the Lenapes' homeland, or 1609, when Henry Hudson explored the Delaware and Hudson rivers.

The Lenapes who watched Hudson drop anchor off Sandy Hook, like their ancestors who so briefly encountered Verrazano, may have been impressed with the Europeans, but they showed no fear. Hudson's first mate wrote both that they seemed "very glad of our coming" and that they quickly boarded the boat to trade "for Knives and Beads."[2] The initial friendliness, however, soon disappeared. Before the Europeans returned to the open sea, one of their crew lay dead with an arrow through his throat—he was buried beneath the sands of New Jersey—and eight to ten Lenapes fell before musket and small cannon fire.

We do not know the cause of the conflict, but we do know that European firepower failed to intimidate the Lenapes. Even after one of their canoes had been destroyed by the ship's cannon, "they manned off another Canoe with nine or ten men," which the Europeans blasted in its turn.[3] Although the Europeans thus defeated the Lenapes in a sea battle, they did not remain to see if the Indians would try again. Instead, they

Interview of Hendrick (Henry) Hudson with the Indians, Seth Eastman. *Henry Hudson's meeting with Indians along the Hudson River, portrayed by Captain Seth Eastman of the United States Army (1808–1875). This imaginative, but on the whole realistic, picture attempts to recapture the moment when the Indians first tasted the Europeans' liquor. Note Hudson passing a cup to the Indian. The peaceful meeting was one of trade, but less peaceful encounters would follow.* SOURCE: HENRY ROWE SCHOOLCRAFT, HISTORY, CONDITIONS AND PROSPECTS OF THE INDIAN TRIBES OF THE UNITED STATES (PHILADELPHIA, 1852), VOL. 2, PLATE 2.

put out to sea. The episode proved that Lenapes who sought to trade, if provoked, were not afraid to fight. It was a lesson that Europeans would learn many times in the next two centuries.

Trade

American Indian women played a critical part in the European colonization of America, a part all too often neglected in our histories, and a part well demonstrated by the Dutch and Swedish experience on the Hudson and Delaware rivers. These Europeans, like the first French and Scottish travelers of the later American West, came to the mid-Atlantic coast primarily to trade. They were not very interested in cultivating the land, nor did they have to be, for Indian women could provide them with corn when supplies ran low. "If no wheat or rye can be had for bread," wrote one proponent of colonization, "maize can always be had from the Indians at a reasonable price." When the Swedes established posts along the Delaware River, they "and other Europeans constantly resorted" to Lenape villages "to purchase Indian corn."[4]

Far from their native lands and unused to their new environment, the Europeans depended on the Lenape women's superior knowledge of American crops during the first generation of colonization. In these early years, Lenape women gladly traded their corn with the Dutch, Swedish, and occasional English newcomers for metal utensils and cloth goods. But the Europeans had not come to *Lenapehoking* to trade for corn alone; they also wanted furs and skins, the produce of Indian men.

Several Dutch explorers traded with the Lenapes in the years following Hudson's voyage. Between 1622 and 1624 the Dutch built trading posts at New Amsterdam (now New York City), and in 1624 they established two posts on the Delaware River, one at Fort Nassau on the Jersey side opposite the mouth of the Schuylkill River, and one at the site of modern Trenton. They abandoned these Delaware posts in 1626, replacing them with a trading craft that cruised the river for furs.

Determined to monopolize the trade with the Indians, the Dutch established another post on the Delaware in 1631. This one, called Swanendael, was on the west bank (near modern Lewes, Delaware). It fell to Lenape warriors within a year, and every colonist was killed. Our only source indicates that the dispute arose after the Indians removed the Dutch coat of arms from a column some distance from the fort. Whatever the issue, the Dutch made peace with the Lenapes and returned to the river in 1633. The Netherlanders strengthened their domination of the Delaware River trade by reoccupying Fort Nassau in 1636, and continued to control the trade until the Swedes established permanent posts in 1638.

Once involved in the trade, the Lenapes became dependent on it. It was not that they needed the luxury of cloth and metal to live, but that they had to have guns, gunpowder and lead to protect them from their enemies. The fur trade not only brought them goods; it brought them deadly competition.

Indians who sought to become involved in the new trade needed access both to furs (or skins) and to European trade goods. Some Indians had the good fortune to be within walking or canoeing distance, through safe territory, of both good hunting grounds and well-stocked trading posts. These hunters simply went upriver to hunt and returned downriver to trade skins for European-made goods at the trading post. Few Lenapes, however, ever had such an ideal position. The three basic conditions of the trade—safe travel, adequate supply of skins, and traders with goods—were rarely all present at once to any one Indian.

In the early years, the Lenapes had access to both traders and furs, but their Delaware River became unsafe for travel when the Susquehannock Indians, then called Minquas, advanced from the interior of Pennsylvania. As early as 1626 the Susquehannocks waged war on them. Instead of hunting, the Lenapes had to spend the hunting seasons defending their villages, "being constantly harassed by war with the Minquaes."[5] In 1633 and 1634 traders reported that war still raged and that the Susquehannocks seemed to be winning. Eventually the Lenapes were deprived of their lands on the west bank of the Delaware.

The 1640s finally brought peace. By then, however, other problems pressed hard on the Lenapes. They had secured their own safety, but the beaver, on which the trade now depended, had been hunted to near extinction in their territory. Beaver still thrived in the Susquehanna River drainage to the west, but this was the Susquehannocks' land and the Lenapes could not hunt there. Instead, they became traders, packing the Susquehannocks' furs across their own lands to New Amsterdam, where goods were plentiful, and then packing Dutch merchandise back to the Susquehannocks to sell for a profit. For a brief period, until the Dutch seized the Swedish posts on the Delaware, the Lenapes enjoyed the role of middlemen in the trade.

War

Trade with the Europeans did not always mean peace with them. This was true throughout colonial North America. Even when the Indians were not invaded openly, they had many grievances against the colonists that could lead to war. Four major issues provided the underlying causes of the Lenapes' wars with the Dutch.

First, though the Dutch and the Lenapes were partners in the trade, they were not allies. The Dutch readily treated and traded with potential enemies of the Lenapes, escalating the Lenapes' need for firearms.

Second, in 1639 the Dutch pushed their settlements beyond lower Manhattan onto Staten Island and into what is now New Jersey. Some Indians thought that their lands were being stolen.

Third, the conflicting agricultural practices of the Lenapes and the Europeans led to trouble. The settlers fenced their grain fields but allowed their cattle and swine to run wild. Livestock often roamed beyond the bounds of European settlement and went "hog wild" in Indian cornfields, destroying essential food supplies. When Indians killed the animals, the Dutch accused them of theft.

Finally, the trade itself created difficulties. It invariably involved debts, and debts often went unpaid.

Differences such as these—in diplomacy, land ownership, land use, and trade—boiled beneath the surface of even friendly European-Indian relations in the mid-seventeenth century. These differences provided the underlying causes for the warfare that erupted between the Munsee-speaking Lenapes of the north and their Dutch neighbors.

Kieft's War (1639–1645)

Many of these grievances burst into the open during Kieft's War, the most serious Indian War that the area would ever experience. Governor Willem Kieft of New Netherland blundered into it when he badly miscalculated the Lenapes' ability and will to resist European aggression. In September 1639, the governor declared that the Indians in the neighborhood of Manhattan, including the Munsee-speakers of what is now New Jersey, had to pay tribute to the Dutch. This came as a shock to the Lenapes, who felt no obligation to bow to Dutch blustering. Lenapes from the Tappan villages told a Dutch trader that "they were very much surprised" that Kieft "dare exact . . . [this tribute]; and he must be a very mean fellow to come to live in this country without being invited by them, and now wish to compel them to give him their corn for nothing."[6]

The spring following Kieft's announcement, a group of Raritan Lenapes attempted to plunder a Dutch trading vessel, ironically named *Peace*. The ship's crew escaped to bring the bad news to the colony. The Raritans were then blamed for stealing hogs on Staten Island, though it later appeared that colonists were at fault. Kieft decided to force the Raritans to submit to Dutch authority. At his orders, Cornelis Van Tienhoven led eighty soldiers to the Raritans' village. He summarily executed four Indians and subjected the peace chief's brother to torture.

Full-scale war did not break out immediately. The Indians may have been waiting until the hunting season ended, so that they could furnish themselves with Susquehannock furs and Dutch arms. Whatever caused the delay, the Raritans did not forget the injury. In June 1641, they struck back, burning a Dutch farm on Staten Island and killing four of the inhabitants—an exact retaliation.

Kieft responded in a way calculated to prevent further Dutch suffering. He offered a bounty of ten fathoms (sixty feet) of wampum (cylindrical beads made from shells, which the Indians valued highly and the Dutch colonists often used as money) to any Indian who would bring him a Raritan's head. Some of the Long Island Indians took up the offer, and the outnumbered

Raritans decided to let the matter drop. Kieft's luck, however, soon ran out.

Against his advice, some Dutch settlers established a village known as Achter Col beside Newark Bay, five hundred yards from the Hackensacks' principal village, in 1642. The settlers were armed with a deed, though apparently they did not have the consent of the majority of neighboring Hackensack Lenapes. The settlement of this village, itself alarming to the Lenapes, was followed by several incidents that increased the friction. Dutch livestock fed upon Indian crops. Colonial traders sold the Lenapes adulterated brandy. Violence was finally triggered when one of the Netherlanders cheated a Hackensack warrior out of a fine beaverskin coat. The warrior vowed to kill the swindler and quickly kept his vow.

The Lenapes, like the Dutch, believed that the killing was a serious affair, but they had their own traditions for dealing with murder. According to Lenape law, a killer's family had to offer the victim's relatives payment to compensate for the loss. The victim's family could refuse payment and demand the death of the killer or another of his family, but the peace chief generally encouraged the acceptance of payment to ease tensions and prevent further bloodshed. Seeking to avoid conflict with the colonists, the Hackensack leaders offered to give the Dutch two hundred fathoms of wampum if they would drop the issue. Kieft, however, followed Dutch law. Treating the Indians as if they were Dutch subjects, he demanded that they surrender the murderer to Dutch courts. They never did.

Kieft soon had an opportunity to demonstrate Dutch power. A Lenape village in what is now Westchester County, New York, was attacked by eighty musket-bearing Mahican Indians. The Lenapes fled and settled as refugees among their Hackensack and Tappan relatives. Kieft, despite the objections of many leading New Netherlanders, took advantage of the confusion and sent two heavily armed companies of soldiers to attack the refugees. One of the parties reached Pavonia, in what is now Jersey City, on the night of February 25, 1643. The soldiers massacred eighty men, women and children. According to our only account of the slaughter,

> Young children, some of them snatched from their mothers were
> cut in pieces before the eyes of their parents, and the pieces

were thrown into the fire or into the water; other babes were
bound on planks and then cut through, stabbed and miserably
massacred, so that it would break a heart of stone; some were
thrown into the river and when the fathers and mothers sought
to save them, the soldiers would not suffer them to come ashore.[7]

Another party of Dutch soldiers slaughtered forty more
Lenapes as they slept at Corlaer's Hook on Manhattan Island.
Indians not killed were shipped to English Bermuda and sold
as slaves. The incidents rank among many other massacres of
Indians as the most disgraceful episodes in American history.

Kieft thought European arms had triumphed, but he soon
faced the results of his arrogant policies. Rarely so united, the
Munsee-speaking Lenapes laid skillful siege to New Netherland.
Dutch settlers fled their farms and trading posts in Brooklyn,
Queens, the Bronx, Staten Island, Newark and even parts of
Manhattan, rushing into the narrow confines of New Amster-
dam's walls, from which they watched the rest of their colony
go up in flames.

"Almost every place is abandoned," wrote eight leading New
Netherlanders to the home government,

> We, wretched people, must skulk with wives and little ones that
> still survive, in poverty together, in and around the fort at
> Manhattans (sic) where we are not safe for even an hour; whilst
> the Indians daily threaten to overwhelm us. . . . The enemy meets
> with scarce any resistance.

They concluded in words that must have stung Kieft, who
had so badly underestimated the Lenapes: "These heathens are
strong in might; they have formed an alliance with seven other
nations; (and) are well provided with guns, powder and lead."[8]

The Lenapes killed every man "they could lay hands on,"
but unlike the Europeans, one observer noted, "I never heard
that they did any harm to the women and children."[9] War raged
for two and a half years. When it ended, the results were
unclear. The Dutch managed to destroy Munsee villages in
Brooklyn and Westchester County, New York, and achieved a
grisly victory at Poundridge, New York (1644), where they again
killed noncombatants. But New Netherland also suffered
dramatically, as many of its people, especially those with resources, fled to Holland. The Lenapes never paid Kieft's tribute,

they never surrendered the murderer, and they never submitted
to any of the Dutch demands that had brought on the war. They
merely agreed, in August 1645, not to resume hostilities. "Kieft's
policy of intimidation had been a failure," according to the
leading authority on the war. "The Indians were neither
eradicated nor permanently cowed into submission."[10]

The home government recalled Kieft to Holland to explain
his mismanagement. His replacement came to a colony whose
weakness he blamed on the war: "Many subjects who possessed
means were necessitated to depart."[11]

Lenape Relations with New Sweden

While the Dutch were trying to impose their will upon the
Lenapes near New York, the Swedes established posts along
the Delaware River. New Sweden was a much smaller and
weaker colony than New Netherland. Its relations with the
Indians were characterized by an uneasy tolerance on the part
of each party. The Swedes angered the Lenapes, it appears, by
taking more land than the Lenapes thought they had granted
them. On the basis of a purchase (for which the deed has
disappeared, if it ever actually existed) the Swedes claimed the
right to both banks of the Delaware River, from what is now
Philadelphia almost to the Atlantic: quite an extensive piece of
real estate. The Lenapes claimed that the Swedes had bought
only a fragment of it—as much as was bordered by "six trees"—
on which "to plant some tobacco." The rest of inhabited New
Sweden, the Lenapes claimed, was stolen.[12]

Troubles between the Unami-speaking Lenapes and the
Swedes had much the same roots as those in the north between
the Munsee-speaking Lenapes and the Dutch: diplomatic disputes, land use differences and trade abuses. These tensions
might have led to warfare as they did in the north. Fortunately
for both parties, the Swedes were ill-equipped for war and thus
could not carry out the same policy of intimidation that had
gotten the Netherlanders into so much trouble.

Governor Johan Printz of New Sweden certainly shared
Kieft's unsavory view of the Lenapes. In 1644 he wrote to his
superiors in Sweden: "Nothing would be better than that a
couple of hundred soldiers should be sent here and kept here
until we broke the necks of all of them." He especially resented

Delaware family (detail from a map by Peter Martensson Lindestron, 1653).
*This drawing may have been produced in response to the curiosity of
Europeans about what American Indians looked like, but it is quite
fanciful. It is difficult to understand how the apparent artist, Peter
Lindestrom, could have drawn such an inaccurate picture when he wrote
with such precision about Lenape appearance.* COURTESY RIKSARKIVET,
STOCKHOLM, SWEDEN.

the Lenapes' successful pursuit of the Susquehannock Indian trade. They were beating Europeans at their own game. If only, he wrote, "I should receive a couple of hundred good soldiers and in addition necessary means and good officers, then with the help of God not a single savage would be allowed to live in this river."[13]

Printz almost certainly underestimated Lenape strength, as Kieft did. But instead of paying in money and blood in a war that would most likely have been as costly and pointless a war as the one which punished New Netherland, the Swedes paid regular tribute to the Lenapes in exchange for the peaceful possession of the land. The tribute, paid in trade goods, furthered the Lenapes' trade with the Susquehannocks.

Despite a number of potentially dangerous incidents, including about eight murders for which the Lenapes atoned with wampum, peaceful relations between the Swedes and the Lenapes lasted until the Dutch, under Governor Peter Stuyvesant, conquered New Sweden in 1655.

Stuyvesant arrived in August of that year and rapidly overran the ill-prepared Swedish colony. While besieging the Swedes at Fort Christina, he learned that the Munsee speakers had again gone to war against the Dutch, and that he was urgently needed in New Amsterdam. He offered the Swedes very liberal surrender terms, and the Swedes, not knowing the cause of his hurry, accepted them. He then sailed back to New Amsterdam to face the colony's second Indian war, known as the "Peach War" because it reportedly began in an orchard.

Killings by both Indians and Dutch had occurred in Manhattan, Staten Island and New Jersey. Understanding that a pointless war had begun once again with Dutch as well as Indian provocation, and perhaps remembering the devastation of the last war, Stuyvesant moved toward negotiation. Although sporadic violence continued, never again would New Jersey see full-scale Indian war. An official peace was finally signed on March 6, 1660.

Disease

New Jersey's Lenapes demonstrated their skills as farmers, hunters, traders, and warriors between the first arrival of the

Dutch in 1624 and the fall of New Netherlands to the English in 1664. They supplied food, without which European settlement might have failed. They outmaneuvered the Swedes in securing the Susquehannock Indians' fur trade, and they demonstrated their military prowess against the Dutch. Still, they fought a long and losing battle against what was clearly their deadliest enemy, disease.

The Europeans and Africans who landed in the Americas between 1492 and 1700 unknowingly brought diseases against which the American Indians had few immunities. These diseases had probably spread throughout Africa, Asia, and Europe after the Bering land bridge disappeared beneath the Arctic waters, isolating the Indians in America. For thousands of years, while old-world populations were developing their resistance to smallpox, tuberculosis and malaria, the Indians had apparently lived free of these killers. This environmental accident is one of the most important factors in both Native American and colonial history, for it meant that when the new peoples arrived from across the Atlantic, Native Americans died. Peter Lindestrom, New Sweden's settler-historian, noted in the 1650s that when a "contagious disease should come into the country, ... whole nations could die out." Thirty years later, Daniel Denton wrote that God showed his favor to the English by killing off the Indians: "Where the English come to settle, a Divine Hand makes way for them, by removing or cutting off the Indians either by Wars one with the other, or by some raging mortal Disease."[14]

How rapidly the Indians succumbed to the new diseases is a matter of depressing debate, but whatever the death rate, it was catastrophic. The Lenapes told Gabriel Thomas in the 1690s that "two of them die to every one Christian that comes in here."[15] In 1640 Indians in the Hudson River Valley claimed that in the twenty years since the Dutch had settled with them their population had declined by ninety percent. These appalling figures are not unique; elsewhere in the Americas similar devastation occurred.

Smallpox, by all reports, claimed the most lives. New Jersey Lenapes fell before at least three raging epidemics of it. The first hit them in the early decades of the seventeenth century. The second caused suffering on an almost unimaginable scale from Chesapeake Bay to the Great Lakes in the 1630s, and the third followed on the heels of the second Dutch war, taking lives throughout the region between 1661 and 1664. Smallpox, as Peter Kalm wrote in 1750, "killed incredible numbers of them."[16] Epidemics of this and other diseases—influenza, malaria, measles, even bubonic plague—swept through Munsee lands in 1679, 1684 and 1690. The Munsee population probably fell by half between 1679 and 1715.

The diseases greatly weakened the Lenapes' ability to resist European aggression as the seventeenth and eighteenth centuries wore on. By 1664, when the English conquered New Netherland, the Dutch population probably already exceeded that of the Lenapes, and troubles in the west had reduced the Indians' ability to maintain their role as middlemen in the fur trade.

Conclusion

Not only did the Lenapes suffer from the disastrous loss of family and friends to disease, but the land around them changed in ways that made their traditional way of life more difficult. The Europeans' livestock continued to run wild, damaging Lenape cornfields. Dutch swine found the region's forests especially attractive. According to one excited New Netherlander: "When the grass is fine, the sows and pigs are driven woodwards to help themselves. At a year old the young sows have pigs. Thus hogs are multiplied, and are plenty in the New Netherlands."[17] As the herds of swine increased, the available food for deer declined. This and the hunting of deer for their skins, by both Europeans and Indians, decreased the number of deer throughout the area.

European expansion, ravaging diseases, increased warfare, and serious ecological changes all threatened the Lenapes' way of life in New Jersey. After the English conquered New Netherland in 1664, the threats grew more alarming.

CHAPTER THREE

Lenapehoking Falls;
The Lenapes Survive, 1664–1801

While the Lenapes were attempting to recover from their third disastrous bout with smallpox, a war between the English and the Dutch brought great changes to *Lenapehoking.* The English, under Sir Richard Nicolls,† put New Amsterdam under the guns of four frigates and conquered the small city without firing a shot. The rest of New Netherland soon yielded to English authority. The transfer of power had dangerous implications for the Lenapes, because the English were far more interested in actually settling the land than the Dutch, who had come to America largely to trade. The Dutch had trickled into New Jersey; the English poured into the colony from nearby Long Island and from New England. Before long, the Lenapes were a minority in their own homeland.

The expansion of European settlement dramatically transformed the Lenapes' world. European lumbermen and settlers, seeking wood for fuel, destroyed much of the forest habitat of deer, bear and wild turkeys. European hunters and livestock drove the deer from the woods that remained. Europeans competed for shellfish; unlike the Lenapes they dug mollusks "at all times of the year," and they dug them to near-extinction. The new settlers even altered the habits of sea fish that had once spawned in New Jersey's rivers. When these fish entered the streams from the ocean, they encountered new mill dams that, in the words of an eighteenth-century observer, "prevent their proceeding," so that "they turn back, and never return."[1]

These ecological changes impaired the Lenapes' means of earning a livelihood.

Weakened by disease and outnumbered by the burgeoning population of the Europeans, the Lenapes could not match the military power of the new settlers. They could not expect to drive them from New Jersey as they had driven out the Dutch in 1643 and 1655.

As the Lenapes came to recognize that they had lost power, they came to disagree among themselves over the causes of loss and the actions they should take to remedy it. Some advocated abandoning their traditions and adopting the ways of the newcomers. This group argued that the Lenapes should learn the secrets of the Europeans' superior power. These Lenapes were supported by some concerned European-Americans, especially missionaries, but they were also strongly opposed by both Indian-hating Europeans and more traditional Lenapes.

The traditionalists believed that their declining power resulted from a failure to live up to the demands of their own culture. Their tradition had not failed them, they believed; they had failed their tradition. The Lenapes could regain power, they declared, by scrupulously performing the old ceremonies and by avoiding the corrupting European influences. These Indians came to argue, moreover, that the European-Americans would never allow Indians to live as equals; that all the attempts of the missionaries to "civilize" them were actually attempts to enslave them. Rather than see their traditions drowned in the torrent of European settlement, these Indians moved west— first to Pennsylvania, and then to the Ohio Country. They did not, however, forget either their origins in *Lenapehoking* or the relatives whom they left behind.

Not all Lenapes, of course, subscribed to either position. Quite a few shifted from one position to the other. Most probably stood somewhere between, accepting many products of European technology and a few European ideas but rejecting the bulk of Western religion, politics and social organization. Yet throughout the eighteenth century those who favored tradition carried on their debate with those who favored the adoption of European ways, and times came when the people in the middle had to take a stand.

In its broad outlines, this debate is not unique in American history. Black American leaders have long disagreed about how far blacks should seek to assimilate with the majority population. Some leaders place their hopes in eventual political, social and economic equality; others seek equality through a separatist black nationalism. Immigrant groups have also debated among themselves both the importance of preserving their particular identities and the best means of doing so. The Lenapes and other coastal Indians simply carried on this very American debate at a very early period.

Lenape Migrations, 1664-1740

The English colonies in southeastern New York, northern New Jersey, and the Delaware Valley avoided war with the Lenapes for three quarters of a century. By the end of that period, in spite of the general peace, Indians constituted less than two-thirds of one percent—a tiny fragment—of New Jersey's population. The high Indian death rate, caused by new diseases and rapidly increasing European immigration, accounted for part of this dramatic population decline, but Lenape emigration to lands west of the Delaware River also contributed to it. Though the Lenapes left New Jersey peacefully, their retreat was not without its tensions. Violent incidents marred relations between them and the English-speaking settlers in colonial New Jersey.

The first region to be heavily settled by the English lay between Sandy Hook and the Raritan River, in the neighborhood of the Navesink Lenapes. Although the English had purchased the lands from Navesink leaders, some Indian warriors plundered the English settlements in 1665. Tensions diminished when Colonel Richard Nicolls, now commander of the British garrison in New York, landed with a strong military force and a generous supply of gifts for cooperative Indians. Nicolls both threatened and bribed, and the Navesink leaders agreed to prevent their warriors from raiding the settlement.

A decade later, the northern New Jersey area felt the disturbing reverberations of Puritan New England's devastating war against its Indians, generally known as King Philip's War. Fearing that the New England Indians might rally the Lenapes, Edmund Andros,† governor of both New York and New Jersey, treated with the peace chiefs of several Munsee-speaking groups, including the Hackensacks. They reassured Andros that

Lappawinsoe. An eighteenth-century Lenape, draped in a trade blanket of English manufacture. The paintings or tattoos on his forehead probably represent figures from Indian myth, perhaps the Thunderbird and Great Horned Serpent common throughout much of North America. The pouch on his chest may contain his "medicine bundle," the sacred, personal items that aided his communication with the spirit world. PORTRAIT BY GUSTAVUS HESSELIUS, COURTESY HISTORICAL SOCIETY OF PENNSYLVANIA.

he had nothing to fear, and they even agreed to leave two warriors with the English as hostages. This "false crisis," writes one historian, "was the last Indian alarm of any consequence" in the greater New York area.[2]

To the south, on the east bank of the Delaware River, the situation was much the same; tensions arose but war was avoided. In 1671, for example, a Lenape from the village of Mantes lost his sister to illness, perhaps to one of the new

Tish-co-han. *This eighteenth-century Lenape chief combines both English and Indian elements in his clothing. The blanket is probably of English manufacture, although Tish-co-han wears it in Indian fashion. The pouch, probably a "medicine bundle" containing items of sacred importance to Tish-co-han, is clearly of Indian origin. PORTRAIT BY GUSTAVUS HESSELIUS, COURTESY HISTORICAL SOCIETY OF PENNSYLVANIA.*

diseases. The grief-stricken warrior was convinced that the English had cast a murderous spell on the woman. He and a companion retaliated, following the Lenape custom of killing two of the enemy's men to avenge the death of one woman. Outraged Europeans threatened the villagers with war. To avoid this, the Mantes leaders agreed to kill the two warriors. One volunteered to die, and they turned his body over to the English. The other apparently escaped, but the issue was dropped.

This incident demonstrates the Lenape anxiety about the European presence. Just as the warrior believed that his sister had died of a European act of witchcraft, other Lenapes may have held Europeans responsible for the decimation of their population. Without being aware of it, the newcomers did bear that responsibility. The incident also shows that the Lenapes did not suffer the catastrophes of disease, ecological change and English expansion without resentment. As one peace chief said, "where the English come they drive ... [the Indians] from their lands."[3]

Although the Lenapes were not driven out with force of arms, their exodus took place only after the rapid English colonization had made life unbearable for most of them. Between 1670 and 1700, while the Lenape population in New Jersey was falling to probably less than six thousand, the European and African population of the colony increased from about one thousand to about fourteen hundred. With their environment changing and disease spreading dramatically, the Indians found their traditional way of life impossible. The colonists were eager to have more territory, and the Lenapes were desperate for goods and unable to maintain themselves under the new conditions. Often willingly, sometimes grudgingly, but generally carefully, they sold their lands and moved west.

The English attempted to appear to act justly in the land transactions. In West New Jersey (which had its own government from 1675 to 1701) officials explicitly recognized the rights of Indians to their lands, and in East New Jersey negotiators recognized them in practice. But the rights only regulated the process by which the English gained Lenape territory; they did not give individual Indians a protected place in colonial society, and they did not look toward the permanent possession of any land by Indians. What they did was to ensure that the colonial governments would regulate purchases of Indian land.

One incident in which the English claimed to act justly was in the trial at Perth Amboy of an influential Lenape, Wequalia. He was charged with murdering a British subject, John Leonard. Lenapes and Britons converged on the court, where Wequalia was found guilty and sentenced to be hanged until dead. He was executed in 1728. Lenapes later claimed that the trial had been unfair, because the court had not adequately considered their charge that Leonard had cheated Wequalia out of valuable

lands. Whatever the merits of the arguments, the murder and
the execution did not improve British-Indian relations in New
Jersey.

While population pressure, diseases, ecological change, and
friction between Europeans and Indians were pushing the
Lenapes out of the colony, other important factors were pulling
them deeper into Pennsylvania. Among these, two stand out.
The first was the vision of harmony between Indians and Europeans held by Pennsylvania governor William Penn.† The
second was the dispersal of the Susquehannock Indians from
central Pennsylvania in the 1670s, which left land open for
settlement by displaced New Jersey Lenapes.

William Penn established his colony in 1682. He scrupulously
purchased the land from the Indians and directed that all
disputes between his colonists and the Indians should be settled
through negotiation, not war. Although he was only briefly in
the colony, his subordinates carried out many of his policies.
In his final years, however, and especially after his death in 1718,
less principled leaders guided colonial policy, and friction developed between the Lenapes and the Pennsylvanians. Lenapes
could move into Pennsylvania during this period largely because
the Susquehannocks' control of the eastern portions of the
region had evaporated.

Until recently, historians believed that the Iroquois Indians
had virtually exterminated the Susquehannocks and had conquered all of the Lenapes sometime before the early eighteenth
century. Recent studies, however, suggest that the Susquehannocks, after suffering defeat by colonists, had voluntarily dispersed themselves among the Lenapes and the Iroquois, leaving
their lands open for settlement. Many of the New Jersey
Lenapes migrated into those lands during the late seventeenth
and early eighteenth centuries. The Iroquois, who claimed the
land, eventually maintained that they had conquered the
Lenapes in war, but little evidence for this has come to light.

Removal and Revival: Lenapes in the West to 1765

The late seventeenth and early eighteenth centuries were
times of migration for the Lenapes. In the early eighteenth
century Lenape villagers continued to inhabit southern New

Jersey, both sides of the Delaware River above Philadelphia, and lands along the Lehigh, the Brandywine, and the Susquehanna rivers in Pennsylvania. By the 1720s, many Lenapes and their increasingly close Shawnee allies had migrated to the Ohio River region, so that within another ten years, Lenapes born in New Jersey were hunting, planting, and trading in lands west of the Appalachian Mountains, remote from Anglo-American settlements. By 1730, the Lenapes lived in three regions: the upper Ohio River Valley, Pennsylvania's Susquehanna and upper Delaware valleys, and the plains of southern New Jersey.

Broadly speaking, these three regional groups had three separate experiences in the mid-eighteenth century. Indians who remained in New Jersey generally sought to adopt Anglo-American ways. Those in eastern and central Pennsylvania became caught, after the death of William Penn, between the diplomatic and military strength of the Iroquois Indians and the economic power of colonial Pennsylvania, and thus lost much of their political independence. Some of these, like those who were still in New Jersey, sought to answer their problems by following the ways of the colonists; others did the reverse, and became deeply involved in movements to revive their traditions. In the third region, the Ohio, the desire to revive and preserve the traditions dominated. Most Ohio Lenapes remained fiercely independent of both the Iroquois and the colonists throughout the eighteenth century.

In general, then, each Lenape group's strategy for survival in the first half of the eighteenth century corresponded with its pattern of settlement. Those who remained in New Jersey and some who migrated west seriously considered the missionaries' offers to teach them the ways of the whites. But most who moved west became determined to reject European religion and authority; the further west they dwelled, the stronger was their determination.

The desire to adhere to tradition remained a potent force among the Lenapes of the Susquehanna and Ohio rivers for years to come and produced several movements of resistance to Anglo-American cultural and military expansion. A Lenape prophet named Neolin† played a critical role in arousing the Indians of the Ohio River and Great Lakes regions during Pontiac's War.† Other Lenapes were at the forefront in battles against Anglo-American expansion from the middle of the eigh-

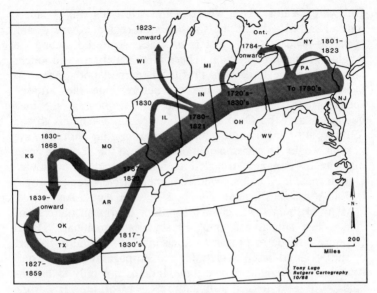

Map, the Lenapes' Roads West. The Lenape migrations, as described in the text. The map does not show the most recent movements. Many Lenape descendants went with the Dust Bowlers to California in the 1930s, and others have taken their own individual roads out of Ontario, Wisconsin, and Oklahoma. SOURCE: HERBERT C. KRAFT, THE LENAPE: SOCIOLOGY, HISTORY, AND ETHNOGRAPHY (NEWARK, 1986).

teenth century until the first decades of the nineteenth. At times during this period they debated both with the Christians in their own groups and with the New Jersey Indians who were attempting to convert to Christianity and to a European way of life.

The Road in the East

Although by the middle of the eighteenth century the European settlers of New Jersey had pushed most of the Lenapes across the Delaware and into Pennsylvania, a small contingent remained in the colony. These Lenapes lived in places that had been only sparsely settled by the Europeans and that remain relatively rural even today: the northwestern portion above the

Delaware Water Gap, where some Munsees still planted, hunted and fished, and the south-central region, where Unami speakers lived in small clusters of shacks scattered among the Anglo-American population. These Unami Lenapes, no longer able to hunt or trade furs profitably, earned poor livings as basket, mat and broom makers. Before long the Munsee speakers and many Unamis would remove west to the Susquehanna and the Ohio region, but scattered Unamis to the south would remain in New Jersey, experimenting with the ways of their Anglo-American neighbors. While to the West the great majority of Lenapes struggled to adhere to their traditions, Unami-speaking Lenapes who remained in New Jersey sought to find a means of living side by side with Anglo-Americans.

Many of them saw a chance to adopt European patterns of living when an earnest young Presbyterian missionary, David Brainerd, arrived to preach to them in 1745. Brainerd, backed by the Scotland-based Society for the Propagation of Christian Knowledge, sought to convert the Indians not only to his religion, but also to his own culture's way of life. His work increased the controversy among Indians over how they should deal with their loss of power to the English-speaking newcomers.

In June of that year, Brainerd's most interested audience gathered at Crosswicks (then sometimes called Crossweeksung or Closeweeksung). Lenapes from throughout southern New Jersey and eastern Pennsylvania migrated to Crosswicks, where they established a small Indian community of about twenty families, numbering at least seventy people. Between one-third and one-half of these Indians convinced Brainerd that they had made true conversions to Christianity. Two of these were Brainerd's Lenape interpreter, Moses Tunda Tatamy,† and an old Lenape religious leader. Tatamy rose to leadership among the New Jersey Lenapes during this period.

Describing the beginnings of the Lenape conversions, Brainerd wrote that after one of his most powerful sermons he "stood amazed at the influence that seized the audience." Not everyone, however, was swept away in the wave of early conversions. Brainerd noted that some Lenapes, far from imitating the converts, preferred "to deride them."[4]

Brainerd also attempted to persuade the Indians to live in a European manner. The men, he believed, should farm; the women should cook, spin, and attend to domestic affairs. To achieve these ends, he and his congregation moved in the spring of 1746 to a more suitable piece of land near Cranbury. There they settled a town, which Brainerd named Bethel. The group now numbered about 130 persons. Together with another group of about twenty Indians at Weepink (now Vincentown), many of whom were also friendly to Christianity, Brainerd's mission probably included the majority of the Indians in the colony.

But all was not well with the Bethel Indians. Alcoholism, a problem among all Indian peoples in the colonies, ravaged the village despite Brainerd's preaching. Another problem was more immediate: the Anglo-Americans of the region did not welcome their new neighbors. Some Cranbury folk complained to the governor that they "were extremely Alarmed, at this Number of Indians Coming to Settle there, where its Esteemed impossible for such a number to live without Stealing or Killing their Neighbours Creatures."[5] Even worse, the townspeople argued that the Bethel Indians were in league with the French in Canada, enemies to the English colonies. As elsewhere, the growing race prejudice of the colonists, the conviction that Indians were and would always be thieves and enemies, reduced the chance that the two peoples could accommodate each other.

David Brainerd died of tuberculosis within the year, depriving the New Jersey Indians of a familiar and capable mediator with the Anglo-Americans. Then, before his younger brother, John Brainerd, arrived to replace him the following year, the 160 Indians were struck with a deadly epidemic. Some declared that this proved the missionaries' religion ineffective, and many Lenapes left the faith.

The mission's most serious problem was that David Brainerd had unwittingly settled it on disputed land. In the late 1740s and early 1750s, New Jersey's chief justice, Robert Hunter Morris, claimed extensive holdings throughout the colony, and he won many of his claims in court. One successful case involved the site of Bethel. The Indians were now landless. By 1753, most of them had left, and the mission had broken up.

A year later, when the French and Indian War (1754–1763) broke out in the West, the government of New Jersey was forced to pay attention to its Indians. The colony's Lenape residents were related to many of the Lenapes in the Susquehanna and Ohio countries who joined the French to resist the expansion of Anglo-American settlement. Late in the spring of 1756, these western Indians and their allies struck deep into the English colonies, raiding Sussex County, New Jersey.

The raid startled and frightened the colonists, and Governor Jonathan Belcher responded quickly by placing bounties on enemy Indian prisoners and scalps, a practice that had become common in the colonies. He offered 150 Spanish dollars for every adult male Indian prisoner, 130 for every female or child, and fifty for every adult male Indian's scalp. To protect the peaceful New Jersey Indians, but perhaps also to keep them from joining their relatives, he advised them to stay close to their homes lest they lose their lives or liberty.

New Jersey's Indians, for their part, continued to seek acceptance among their Anglo-American neighbors. Some of them even served in the British forces. Twenty New Jersey Lenapes were captured by the enemy at the bloody siege of Fort William Henry on New York's northern frontier in 1757. As John Brainerd later wrote, "The Indians have, every year since the commencement of the war, enlisted into the King's service far beyond ... proportion, and generally more or less every campaign have died in the Army."[6]

This imbalance conforms to a broad pattern: Poor minorities, and particularly Indians, have served and died in America's wars in greater proportion to their numbers than have Americans of European descent. The Lenapes would repeat the performance during the Civil War a century later.

Enemy forces raided the colony again in 1757 and 1758. By the spring of 1758, twenty-seven settlers in the northwestern parts had been killed. Although the raiders were western Indians, the government grew concerned about the Indians living in New Jersey. The government distrusted the Lenapes despite their military service; after all, their relatives in the west continued to raid the colony.

Outside the government, meanwhile, groups which sincerely sought to aid the Indians, such as the Society of Friends' New Jersey Association for Helping the Indians and John Brainerd's Scottish Society for the Propagation of Christian Knowledge, encouraged the government to take positive action concerning the New Jersey Lenapes. If they could be brought to a European way of living, Friends and Presbyterians argued, they would become good subjects and the peace would be preserved. Thus two very different impulses—the one of hostile fear and the other of paternalistic philanthropy—combined to drive New Jersey's government toward a solution to the Indian problem.

By October 1758, the colony had taken two important steps. First, it purchased the remaining claims of twenty-eight important Susquehanna River Lenapes, most of them from the Minisink and Oping bands, that held lands in northern New Jersey. Interestingly, the Indians seem to have retained the right to hunt and gather on these lands—a right that whites ignored until the 1830s. Second, the government dealt with those who remained in New Jersey. In August 1758, it purchased a tract of land in the Burlington County pinelands to be held and protected for the Indians' exclusive use. In exchange, five leaders of southern New Jersey bands agreed to give up their claims to properties south of the Raritan River. How the leaders were selected is unclear, but they signed the agreement in September, and the Brotherton Indian Reservation was established.

The new governor, Francis Bernard, believed that the action satisfied "both parties." New Jersey promised not only to hold the land "in trust for the Indians" but also to "build a Town for them," complete with a gristmill. The Indians promised not only to give up their land claims but also to move to the reservation in the pinelands, where they would be "out of the Way of Communication with the wilder Indians"—in other words, where they would be isolated from their relatives in the West, the enemies of New Jersey.[7]

By June 1759, almost two hundred of New Jersey's approximately three hundred Indians had moved to the Brotherton Reservation. There they found a working sawmill, "which serves to provide them with timber for their own use & to raise a little money for other purposes."[8] One of the ten Anglo-American–style frame houses that the government had planned to build was finished and another was under construction.

That month Governor Bernard visited the Indians, held council with their leaders, and "assured them that the same care of them should be continued." Although Bernard never again mentioned the gristmill that his government had promised to build on the reservation, he later reported to his British superiors that the Lenape leaders had expressed their satisfaction with conditions at Brotherton. He also wrote: "If I can but keep them from being supplied with rum, for which there are laws strict enough, I shall hope to make them orderly & useful Subjects."⁹ To make them orderly and useful, the governor meant to make them live an Anglo-American, Christian way of life. Some Indians, it seems, agreed with Bernard that to adopt European customs would insure the survival of their people. To help them make the change, John Brainerd renewed his mission in 1759. He brought promises of support from the government and some immediate support from the Scottish Society for the Propagation of Christian Knowledge.

Brainerd did his best to encourage the Indians to conform to his vision of the civilized, Christian life. Men, not women, he believed, should plant and tend the fields. Women should remain at home, spinning cloth from flax. With the profits the men would make from operating the sawmill and raising crops, the women could purchase household items and flax for clothes. Shelter would soon be provided by the government; food would come from the fields and animal pastures. This hopeful vision ran quickly into trouble. To begin with, the population of Brotherton steadily declined. Disease may have been a factor, but Brainerd reported no more epidemics. It is more likely that Lenapes either returned to their scattered homes in south Jersey once the tensions of the French and Indian war had subsided or headed west to resume their traditional way of life among their non-Christian relatives.

Whatever the cause, the population of Brotherton was little more than one hundred Indians by August 1761. About forty more still lived at Cranbury, and about forty remained at Weep-ink. Christian Lenapes lived at all three villages. Within a few years the reservation's sawmill burned. Deprived of income, the Brotherton population sagged to a low of about sixty persons. That year Weepink had only twenty.

Another reason Brainerd's hopes for a Europeanized, Christian Lenape village at Brotherton faltered was that the colonial government never carried out its promises to construct the town. With no financial resources and few material ones, most Lenapes could not make the transition from Lenape to European patterns of living.

The reservation suffered its severest blow, however, during the American Revolution. By breaking off New Jersey's relations with Britain, the war cut off the trickle of funds from the

Scottish Society for the Propagation of Christian Knowledge. Moreover, the violent struggles within the state disrupted life so thoroughly that John Brainerd left the mission to be closer to his relatives in Deerfield, New Jersey. There he remained until his death in 1781. Conditions at Brotherton deteriorated, and basic human needs for food and clothing went unsatisfied.

The Brotherton Indians held on to their reservation until 1801, when forty-six of the sixty-three remaining adults voted to disband the reservation. It was divided into 100-acre tracts and sold by the government to the public. The profits went to the Indians. Seventy of the 100 to 120 Brotherton Lenapes then left the state. This group, the last large body of Lenapes to leave, headed toward a Christian Indian community in New Stockbridge, New York.

CHAPTER FOUR

Westward and Eastern Migration, 1750 to Today

Lenapes in the Old Northwest

Influential Western Lenapes followed a different path than their New Jersey relatives. While many Lenapes in New Jersey and some in Pennsylvania embraced Christianity in the middle decades of the eighteenth century, traditionalist Lenapes along Pennsylvania's Susquehanna River developed a new theory of religion and nationality. This theory recognized the power of European ways but declared that those ways were not for Indians. Just before the outbreak of the French and Indian War some Susquehanna River Lenapes explained the notion to John

Brainerd. The Creator, they said, had made the Indians, Africans, and Europeans separately: "The white man was the youngest brother, and therefore the white people ought not to think themselves better." The Creator, they continued, had given the Bible to the Europeans, instructing them "to worship by that," but had not given books to the Africans or Indians, "and therefore it could not be right for them to have a book or be concerned with that way of worship."[1]

Brainerd noted that the traditionalist Lenapes profoundly distrusted the Anglo-Americans. They suspected that "the white people were contriving a method to deprive them of their country as they had done by the sea side, and to make slaves of their children: as they did of Africans."[2]

Although these Western Lenapes rejected the Presbyterian mission, they maintained an interest in their Christian relatives back in New Jersey. Brainerd wrote in 1751: "They are now, many of them, waiting to see how it fares with their brethren who are becoming Christians, and whether they are in better condition than themselves who remain heathen." In the same year the Lenapes on the Susquehanna invited the New Jersey Lenapes to come west to join them but refused to extend the invitation to the missionaries, for "if one white man came, another would desire it, etc., and so by-and-by they should lose their country."[3]

In 1767 the Western Lenapes, who by then had become concentrated in the upper Ohio River region, repeated the invitation. This time, apparently, Brainerd would be allowed to come along. The Christian Lenapes would have their own Ohio Country village. The Brotherton Indians had enough difficulties to make them seriously consider the offer. They decided against it however, when their interpreter, Joseph Peepy, returned from a visit to the West with discouraging accounts that included rumors of war.

Between 1768 and the outbreak of the American Revolution the Western Lenapes divided over how to deal with continued Anglo-American expansion. One group, headed by White Eyes† and John Killbuck, Jr.,† sought to accommodate the Anglo-Americans. In 1771, Killbuck, himself periodically attracted to Christianity, journeyed east to invite the New Jersey Indians, once again, to move west. Such a move would have increased support for Killbuck's policies of accommodation.

Because White Eyes and Killbuck faced strong and dangerous opposition from their own people, the Brotherton Lenapes determined to stay in the East. It was probably a wise decision. The American Revolution broke out, bringing with it an Indian war in the West. Had the Brotherton Lenapes been in the region, they might have suffered the fate of Gnadenhutten and Salem, two Moravian Christian Indian villages there. Although these villages were friendly to the Americans, Pennsylvania militiamen attacked them on March 8, 1782, and slaughtered ninety-six Lenapes—men, women and children—in cold blood.

Until the killings at Gnadenhutten the Americans had hoped the Ohio Lenapes would be neutral. Now, the Lenapes became devoted enemies of the young United States. Even after the British had given up the fight in 1781, Lenapes and other Western Indians continued their war. By the 1790s, that war had become one of defense, as Americans moved to the Ohio Country. In 1790 and 1791, the combined forces of Lenapes and other Ohioan tribes threw back two invading American armies.

The second of these Indian victories, the annihilation of the numerically superior American army under Arthur St. Clair,† now stands as the worst defeat ever suffered by an Indian-fighting American army. Twenty Indians were killed and forty were wounded, but 640 Americans died, some four hundred were wounded or captured, and only four hundred made it back to the safety of an American fort. By comparison, George Armstrong Custer lost only 260 men at the more famous battle of the Little Big Horn in 1876.

Despite their two military victories, the Indians could not compete with the vast resources of the United States. Under the very careful generalship of "Mad" Anthony Wayne,† the young republic defeated the Ohio Indians in 1794 at the Battle of the Fallen Timbers. The following year the Lenapes signed away most of their Ohio lands to the American government.

They resettled in two neighboring regions, northwestern Ohio and eastern Indiana. They remained deeply disturbed, however, over their loss of lands. As a result, many of them became followers of a new religious leader, the half-blind Shawnee Prophet.†

The prophet was a Shawnee Indian who lived among the eastern Indiana Lenapes in the early 1800s. He experienced

religious visions that carried a political message. Like the
Delaware Prophet of the 1760s, the Shawnee Prophet urged
his followers to reject the teachings of the Christian missionaries, to abandon specified evil European practices such as
the consumption of alcohol, and to refuse to sell lands to
Americans. Not only did he oppose American land-seekers, he
also opposed Indians who cooperated too closely with the
Americans.

In 1805 he brought accusations of witchcraft against two
Lenape leaders who opposed him. They had signed several
treaties with land speculators, ceding valuable lands. Amid a
storm of controversy, Lenape followers of the Prophet put one
of the two chiefs and some others to death.

These slayings played a critical role in the tribe's politics for
the next decade. A great many Lenapes recoiled from the
action, and increasing numbers rejected the Prophet. As the
United States pushed to acquire more Indian lands, the
Shawnee Prophet and his skillful brother, Tecumseh,† organized
an intertribal resistance. The Lenape leadership declined to
join. Fighting broke out between the Americans and Tecumseh's
confederated tribes in 1811, and merged with the broader War
of 1812. Most Lenapes remained aloof from it, and a few even
worked for the United States.

As White Eyes and Killbuck had learned, however, and as
future generations of Lenapes would also learn, keeping the
peace with the Americans, even cooperating actively with them,
did not save the land from them. Within fifteen years of the
end of the War of 1812, the Americans began urging the
Lenapes to sell their lands and migrate west of the Mississippi
River.

Four Roads West, 1800 to Today

Between 1776 and 1815, the already divided Lenapes broke
up and re-formed into four main groups, each with its own
pattern of migration. These groups spread out ahead of the first
wave of Anglo-American settlement, each seeking a region of
calm.

New Jersey's Brotherton Lenapes, who left the state in 1801, migrated to the Stockbridge Indian Reservation in New York. By the early 1820s, Americans were pressing them once again, and they headed west to the Stockbridge-Munsee Reservation in Wisconsin. Today, about six hundred descendants of these Indians share the reservation's sixteen thousand acres with the descendants of other migrants from the East. Over six hundred other Lenapes hold membership in the Stockbridge-Munsee tribe.

The other three groups lived in the Ohio Country during the American Revolution and separated afterwards. One consisted of Christianized Munsees, Unamis, and other Indians from Gnadenhutten and Salem—the two Moravian villages attacked by Pennsylvania militiamen in the spring of 1782. Shortly before the massacres, traditionalist Lenapes and other Indians had captured the Moravian missionaries, whom they distrusted, and taken them to live near the British fort of Detroit, Michigan. After the massacres the scattered Indian survivors made their way to Michigan. They settled briefly with the missionaries, but during the next few years about 150 of them migrated further, to the Thames River region of Ontario, Canada. There they established Muncy Town and Moraviantown. About four hundred of their descendants still live in Ontario.

In the turbulent years of the late eighteenth century, another group of Lenapes gave up the struggle for the Ohio Country and migrated to the Cape Girardeau region of Missouri. The largest body to break off from the Ohio Lenapes, they became known as the "Absentee Delawares." These people pioneered the trans-Mississippi West for the other Lenapes. But in doing so, they incurred the understandable resentment of the original inhabitants of the region, particularly the Osage Indians.

The Absentee Delawares, though they hoped to escape the expansion of the United States, actually helped pave the way for it by warring with the eastern plains peoples. When the wars with the Osages slacked off, the threat from American settlers increased again. Some of the disgusted Absentees headed southwest to settle the Red River Valley of Arkansas and Oklahoma; they later moved on to Texas, where they obtained a small reservation on the Brazos River to share with other

Native Americans. Another group of Absentees eventually re-joined the main body of Lenapes, who were in Kansas in the 1830s and 1840s.

By the late nineteenth century, the rest of the Absentees had made their way to western Oklahoma, which currently, of all regions, has the largest concentration of descendants of the Absentee Delawares. Today, about a thousand people in Andarko County, Oklahoma, claim descent from Absentee Delawares. Officially known as the Delawares of Western Oklahoma, the Andarko County Lenapes own land privately and share about 300 common acres with the Caddo and Wichita Indians. Although few of these Lenapes either claim full Lenape descent or speak the original language, they have recently organized to preserve and recapture aspects of their traditional culture.

The fourth group of Lenapes, the main body, also wound up in Oklahoma, although by a different route and through different circumstances. These Lenapes struggled to stay on in the Ohio Country, even after the Moravians and Absentees left. They fought against the United States in the late eighteenth century, hoping to keep the government from taking their lands, and then allied with the nation during the War of 1812 in the hope of winning American friendship. Neither policy worked. By 1820, the United States government was pressing the Lenapes to leave the Great Lakes–Ohio Valley region for the trans-Mississippi West.

This migration took place under the supervision of the Department of War. After exchanging their Indiana and Ohio lands for lands claimed by both the United States and the Osage Indians, over 800 Lenapes crossed the Mississippi River in 1820 and 1821. Many children and adults died along the way. Provisions supplied by the government proved inadequate. Hunger, measles and pneumonia plagued the refugees.

They settled beside the White River in Missouri. Their stay proved neither happy nor long. Both white settlers, on the one hand, and Osage Indians, on the other, claimed to own the lands promised to the Lenapes by the United States. They felt pressed between the two groups. The unfamiliar environment posed other difficulties. The fertile soils promised good harvests, but unexpected and extensive flooding ruined the Lenapes' first attempts to plant in the unfamiliar land. Furthermore, the game with which they had hoped to supplement their crops was scarce, because the Osages and whites had already thoroughly hunted the region. By the end of the decade, Lenape leaders had decided that their people might be better off elsewhere. In 1829 and 1830, after negotiating another treaty with the government, the Lenapes left Missouri and moved to Kansas.

They settled towns in what later became Leavenworth and Wyandotte counties. Their reservation had two parts, a large rectangle of over nine hundred thousand acres in eastern Kansas and another nine hundred thousand acres in a narrow strip across much of what is now the state. The United States guaranteed their possession of these lands. With so much land and the guarantee of possession, the reservation attracted other Lenapes, including a small group who had remained in Ohio.

Unfortunately for the Indians, pressures for these lands were not long in coming. In 1854 the United States established a territorial government for Kansas, and white settlers rushed in to form counties in the region south of the Lenape reserve. In Washington, meanwhile, railroad and government officials debated various routes for a transcontinental railroad, some of which would have crossed Lenape land.

While the Lenapes pondered these developments, the white citizens of Kansas quarreled with one another over whether to allow slavery in the territory. For two years an ugly civil conflict, which gave the territory the name of "Bleeding Kansas," foreshadowed the American Civil War.

The Civil War postponed plans for a railroad and temporarily quieted any talk of removing Indians from Kansas. The Lenapes allied with the Union and sent volunteers to war in staggering numbers. In the first year and a half of fighting, half the Lenapes of military age enlisted. An Army officer thought it the largest percentage of volunteers that any social group furnished the Union during that time.

The Lenapes' support for the Union cause did not prevent pressure for their removal from Kansas once the war had ended. A little over a year after General Robert E. Lee surrendered at Appomattox, the Lenapes reluctantly agreed to break up their Kansas reserve. The agreement presented the Lenapes with a difficult choice. They could remain in Kansas as individual landholders with rights to full ownership of eighty acres and with American citizenship, but without membership in an organized, nationally recognized Indian community. Alternatively, they could move to Oklahoma as members of a Lenape community within the Cherokee Nation, with rights to 160 acres of Cherokee land. Most Lenapes chose to move.

About one thousand Lenapes arrived in the Cherokee Nation in 1868 and settled near Dewey, Oklahoma. Known as the Cherokee-Delawares, they retained much of their own political and cultural identity for about two generations. Today their descendants remain the largest single body of Lenapes in North America.

While the Cherokee-Delawares adjusted to their new way of life within the Cherokee Nation, American settlers quickly occupied lands surrounding the area. As the nineteenth century drew to a close, pressures for the "opening" of the Cherokee Nation to American settlement intensified.

Through most of the nineteenth century, the federal government had generally negotiated the removal of Indians from lands it desired by offering the Indians both payment and federal protection on more distant lands that were unoccupied by American citizens. But by 1900, few such lands remained. The government turned instead, then, to another method of obtaining Indian land, a method known as "allotment."

Until late in the nineteenth century reservation Indians generally owned their lands as a group under federal guarantee. No individual could purchase these lands; only the government and the Indian nation could negotiate for them. Eventually, however, Congress replaced this system with allotment. Allotment meant the breaking up of reservation lands, owned collectively by the tribe, into small plots of land, owned individually. Reservation lands, in other words, were allotted to individual members. This policy was intended to woo the Indians away from their tribes, to "Americanize" them, to grant them citizenship, and to have them blend in with the general population. However, it had the ultimate effect of making it easy for white settlers to purchase the alloted lands cheaply.

Allotment came to the Cherokee Nation (and thus to the Cherokee-Delawares) with the move toward Oklahoma statehood between 1898 and 1907. It ended the collective ownership of land and permitted non-Indians to accumulate Indian lands rapidly, destroying the economic and political foundations of Cherokee and Cherokee-Delaware culture.

The Oklahoma Lenapes, however, have retained a certain consciousness of their identity. They have recently demonstrated this in their legal battles, particularly those undertaken since the establishment of the Indian Claims Commission after World War II. Lenapes of western and eastern Oklahoma have worked together to obtain a more just financial settlement for the lands out of which their ancestors were forced in the nineteenth century. The federal courts have awarded them over $9 million. Divided among nine thousand descendants in the mid-1970s, the fund provided over a thousand dollars to each individual. Such a sum, though significant, can only raise questions about whether centuries of suffering can be adequately compensated by court settlements alone.

Besides demonstrating the tenaciousness of the Lenapes, the court battles have provided us with figures for today's Lenape population. Although these figures are incomplete—they include only those descendants of Lenapes whose ancestors migrated to Oklahoma and therefore neglect the descendants of the many Lenapes who did not follow that path of migration—they do give us some idea of where the descendants of the original New Jersey Indians now live. The figures, it should be noted, refer to individuals who claim some Lenape ancestry; very few living Indians claim to descend only from Lenapes.

Of the eight states that list fifty or more Lenapes, all are *west* of the Mississippi River. The vast majority of Lenapes now live over a thousand miles from the Atlantic Ocean. Oklahoma has the largest number. Places along the Lenape migration routes—Arkansas, Kansas, Missouri and Texas—also have significant Lenape populations.

Strikingly, there are over eight hundred descendants of Lenapes on the West Coast, a full continent away from their homeland. Many of these came from families that migrated with the Dust Bowlers from Oklahoma to California during the Great Depression of the 1930s.

The great majority of Lenape descendants, then, live far away from their ancestors' Atlantic homeland. In addition, two other patterns must be counted in the history of New Jersey's Indians: first, the little-known story of the Lenapes who remained in the state; and second, the complicated story of Native Americans from other regions who have migrated to find work in New Jersey since the middle of the nineteenth century.

The East: New Jersey's Indians, 1800 to Today

New Jersey's only Indian reservation broke up, as we have seen, in 1801. Most, about seventy, of the Brotherton Indians emigrated from the state that year. What became of the remaining thirty to fifty, and what became of the unknown numbers of Lenapes who lived in the neighborhoods of Weepink, Crosswicks and Cranbury, is uncertain. Many undoubtedly remained in the state. Throughout the nineteenth century, reports that the descendants of the Brotherton Indians still resided in New Jersey appeared in print and took on the character of a tradition. Some New Jerseyans alive today have been raised with the conviction that they have Lenape ancestors.

These assertions raise problems for scholars. Their validity is often difficult to establish because many Indians have adopted Anglo-American naming practices, and because the census takers did not ask New Jerseyans if they had Native American forebears until the 1890 census. When the question first appeared, eighty-four individuals placed themselves in the Indian category; unfortunately, their tribal affiliations were not recorded.

By the 1890s, New Jersey's expanding industries were attracting workers from around the globe, including some Indians from other parts of the continent. In the census of 1910, sixty-two of the 168 New Jersey Indians reported that they were Sioux, members of a Great Plains tribe. These Indians apparently performed with a Wild West Show that toured American and European cities at the turn of the century, performing much of the time in New York. Although their reason for living in New Jersey was unusual, they do represent a trend in twentieth-century American Indian life: the movement from traditional homelands and reservations to urban areas.

Similarly, some of the "Sand Hill Indians," who lived in what is now the town of Neptune from about 1877 to the middle of this century, also came from outside the state. Other Sand Hill people claimed Lenape descent. These people, who participated in the development of the Jersey Shore as a recreational area, occupied about fifteen acres and maintained an awareness of their traditional ceremonies.

Today, almost fifteen thousand New Jerseyans identify themselves as Native Americans. Most of them, however, are not

Lenapes. Census publications do not record tribal affiliations, and the census of 1990 has not yet been fully released. But the pattern of Native American movement to New Jersey from other areas is clear in the census of 1980. Of the 8,394 Native Americans recorded there, 3,868 apparently had roots in Latin America, and another 218 claimed to be Eskimos or Aleuts with roots in the Arctic or sub-Arctic. There is no way of knowing how accurate these claims are, but the census figures seem to indicate that a very large proportion of the state's Native Americans live far from their ancestral homelands.

The state's Indians bear a legacy of poverty and discrimination. Unemployment and economic hardship trouble a much greater proportion of the state's Indians than whites. While six percent of whites lived below the "poverty line" in 1980, sixteen percent of the Indians did. The poorest lived in the urban centers of Essex, Hudson, and Union counties. Over a quarter of Native Americans in these counties, and a full forty-six percent of those in Jersey City, did not then earn what the federal government defined as a sufficient income.

Despite this poverty, however, the striking fact is that Native Americans have endured. Today, Indians are among the fastest growing groups in the nation. Contrary to romantic fiction, they have not vanished. Indeed, the percentage of New Jerseyans identifying themselves as Indians almost doubled in the 1980s, rising by 78 percent. This astonishing increase cannot be explained either by births or by immigration. Thousands of New Jerseyans called themselves Indians in 1990 who did not in 1980. In other words, the increase may say as much about changing perceptions of what it means to be Indian as it does about changing population. What the figures do tell us is that pride in Indian ancestry is increasing. But the fact of survival and the recent resurgence of Native America cannot disguise past hardships. It is a testament to the appalling population losses that Indians have suffered since the arrival of the first Europeans, and particularly before 1900, that the number of people of Lenape descent, now spread across the continent, has only recently passed conservative estimates of the Lenape population at the time when Giovanni de Verrazano first glimpsed the "densely populated" shores of *Lenapehoking* during his brief encounter in 1524.

CONCLUSION

Struggles for survival dominate the history of New Jersey Indians since their first meeting with Europeans. The struggles to preserve their traditional culture in the face of the European intrusion, the struggles to hold their lands in the face of European invasion, and the struggles to preserve their very lives in the face of dispossession, disease and war: these dismal battles for fundamental human needs fill much of the past four centuries of Lenape history.

Europeans and European-Americans have sometimes lamented the Indians' suffering. Even the soldiers who drove the Indians before them expressed their admiration for the Indians' bravery. But whatever respect the Dutch, British and American officials have had for the Indians, the result of their policies has been the taking of Indian lands.

Looking back over the centuries, some argue that it was all necessary, that the Indians had to lose their lands in order for the American Republic to emerge and gain strength. Some also suggest that, with more modern agricultural and industrial technology, European-American "civilization" can provide more wealth for more people than the American Indian cultures could. Both of these arguments assume, however, that ends justify means, that the goal of a prosperous America justified the exploitation of the land's original inhabitants. Ironically, it is one of the most cherished virtues of our constitutional system that ends do not justify means, that all legal and electoral affairs must be handled with due process, that justice is as justice does. By this standard, Indians saw little justice in the face of the European-American advance.

The tragedy of Indian history is not only compelling for its own sake. It is also instructive. The American Indians continue struggling to defend their cultures and to secure their rights; so do many Americans of all backgrounds work to find ways to accommodate justly the wants and needs of our nation's diverse citizenry. One venerable Lenape woman, Nora Thompson Dean,† recently asked that young Americans reflect upon her people's history. "I want these young people," she said, "to discuss what was done by my departed Delaware people. Many things cannot be done again but can be remembered, the things that the Lenapes did when they lived toward the east long ago."[1]

Only recently have historians attempted to see Native American history as the Indians who experienced it saw it. The attempt to see from Indian points of view (and it is important to remember that Indians have always differed among themselves) gives us a fuller comprehension of what happened. It also trains us to be more understanding, at home and abroad, of all cultures. It helps us to shed our prejudices, so that when we encounter people and ways that seem strange to us, we can see them with our "naked eyes."

NOTES

Full citations are found in "Sources," p. 75.

Introduction

1. Pastorius, "Circumstantial Geographical Description of Pennsylvania (1700)," 420.

Chapter One

1. Kraft, "Indian Prehistory," 7.
2. de Laet, "From the New World," 57.
3. Waubuno, *Traditions of the Delawares,* 14.
4. Penn, "Letter to the Free Society of Traders," 314–15.
5. Van der Donck, *New Netherland,* 21.
6. Zeisberger, "North American Indians," 132.
7. Van der Donck, *New Netherland,* 107–09.
8. Heckewelder, *History, Manners, and Customs of the Indian Nations,* 254.
9. Williams, "Language of America," 115–16; Zeisberger, "North American Indians," 16.
10. Penn, "Letter to the Free Society of Traders," 313.
11. Van der Donck, *New Netherland,* 77; Lindestrom, *Geographia Americae,* 195–96.
12. Van der Donck, *New Netherland,* 84.
13. Speck, *Delaware Indian Big House Ceremony,* 52–53.
14. Harrington, *Religion and Ceremonies of the Lenape,* 73–74.
15. Lindestrom, *Geographia Americae,* 207.
16. Kalm, *Travels in North America,* 229–30.
17. Wassenaer, "Description and First Settlement," 21.
18. Van der Donck, *New Netherland,* 45.
19. Schoolcraft, *Archives of Aboriginal Knowledge,* 6:661.
20. McCullough, "Narrative of Captivity," 289.
21. Schoolcraft, *Archives of Aboriginal Knowledge,* 6:661; Speck, *Naskapi,* 20.

22. Van der Donck, *New Netherland,* 87.
23. Van der Donck, *New Netherland,* 87.
24. Quoted in Harrington, *Religion and Ceremonies of the Lenape,* 56.
25. Quoted in Harrington, *Religion and Ceremonies of the Lenape,* 25.
26. Van der Donck, *New Netherland,* 106.
27. Harrington, *Religion and Ceremonies of the Lenape,* 27; Van der Donck, *New Netherland,* 102.
28. Van der Donck, *New Netherland,* 102; Harrington, *Religion and Ceremonies of the Lenape,* 43.

Chapter Two

1. Wroth, *Voyages of Giovanni de Verranzano,* 137.
2. Juet, *Juet's Journal,* 28.
3. Ibid., 36.
4. "Information respecting Land in New Netherland," 369.
5. "Letter from Issack de Rasiere to the Directors of the Amsterdam Chamber," 211.
6. de Vries, "From the 'Korte Historiael'," in *Narratives of New Netherland,* 209.
7. "Extracts from a work called Breeden Raedt," 4:103–4.
8. "Memorial of the Eight Men," 139–40.
9. "Extracts from a work called Breeden Raedt," 104.
10. Trelease, *Indian Affairs in Colonial New York,* 83.
11. "Report of Peter Stuyvesant (1665)," 365.
12. Jennings, *Ambiguous Iroquois Empire,* 117.
13. "Report of Governor Johan Printz," 103–04.
14. Lindestrom, *Geographia Americae,* 45.
15. Thomas, "An Historical and Geographical Account," 344.
16. Kalm, *Travels in North America,* 258–59.
17. Van der Donck, *New Netherlands,* 42.

Chapter Three

1. Kalm, *Travels in North America,* 154.
2. Trelease, *Indian Affairs in Colonial New York,* 193.
3. Pomfret, *West New Jersey,* 59.
4. *Diary of David Brainerd,* 207, 217–19.
5. "State of the Facts about the Riots," 406.
6. Brainerd, *Life of John Brainerd,* 314.
7. "Letter from Governor Bernard (October 31, 1758)," 140–41.
8. "Letter from Governor Bernard (June 15, 1759)," 175.
9. Ibid., 174–76.

Chapter Four

1. Brainerd, *Life of John Brainerd,* 234–35.
2. Ibid.
3. Ibid., 249, 236.

Conclusion

1. Kriss, "Indians Return to a Spiritual Home."

SOURCES

Introduction

Francis Daniel Pastorius, "Circumstantial Geographical Description of Pennsylvania (1700)," in *Narratives of Early Pennsylvania, West New Jersey, and Delaware, 1630–1707,* ed. Albert Cook Myers (New York, 1912), 353–448

Chapter One

Marshall Becker, "The Lenape Bands Prior to 1740: The Identification of Boundaries and Processes of Culture Change Leading to the Formation of the 'Delawares,' " in *The Lenape Indian: A Symposium,* ed. Herbert C. Kraft (South Orange, N.J., 1984), 19–32

T. J. Brasser, "Early Indian-European Contacts," in Bruce Trigger, ed., *Handbook of North American Indians,* vol. 15: *Northeast* (Washington, D.C., 1978), 78–88

Daniel G. Brinton, *The Lenape and Their Legends* (1894; reprint ed., New York, 1969)

William Cronon, *Changes in the Land: Indians, Colonists and the Ecology of New England* (New York, 1983)

Jaspar Dankers and Peter Sluyter, "Journal of a Voyage to New York, 1679–1680," *Memoirs of the Long Island Historical Society,* trans. Henry C. Murphy, 1 (1867), 1–440

John de Laet, "From the 'New World' " in *Narratives of New Netherland 1609–1664,* ed. J. Franklin Jameson (New York, 1909), 29–60

Isaack de Rasieres, "Letter of Isaack de Rasieres to Samuel Blommaaert, 1628" in *Narratives of New Netherland,* 97–113

David Pietersz DeVries, "From the 'Korte Historiael Inde Journaels Aenteyckeninge' " in *Narratives of Early Pennsylvania,* 1–29

John Ettwein, "Some Remarks and Annotations Concerning the Traditions, Customs, Languages & c. of the Indians in North America," in *Miscellaneous Papers of the Historical and Philosophical Society of Ohio,* microfilm, Glenn A. Black Archaeological Laboratory, Indiana University, Bloomington, Ind

James E. Fitting, "Regional Cultural Development, 300 B.C. to A.D. 1000," in *Handbook, Northeast,* 44–57

Regina Flannery, *An Analysis of Coastal Algonquian Agriculture* (Washington, D.C., 1939)

Robert E. Funk, "Post-Pleistocene Adaptations," in *Handbook, Northeast,* 16–27

Ives Goddard, "Delaware" and "Eastern Algonquian Languages," in *Handbook, Northeast,* 213–39, 70–77

Goddard, "The Delaware Language, Past and Present," in *A Delaware Indian Symposium,* ed. Herbert C. Kraft (Harrisburg, Pa., 1974), 103–10

M. R. Harrington, *Religion and Ceremonies of the Lenape* (New York, 1921)

John Heckewelder, *History, Manners, and Customs of the Indian Nations Who Once Inhabited Pennsylvania, and the Neighboring States* (Philadelphia, 1876)

Thomas Campanius Holm, "A Short Description of the Province of New Sweden, Now Called, by the English, Pennsylvania," in *Memoirs of the Historical Society of Pennsylvania* 3 (1834), 13–166

Ake Hultkrantz, "Feelings for Nature Among North American Indians," and "The Owners of the Animals in the Religion of the North American Indians," in Hultkrantz, *Belief and Worship in Native North America,* ed. Christopher Vescey (Syracuse, 1981), 117–34, 135–46

Peter Kalm, *Travels in North America, 1750,* ed. Adolph B. Benson (New York, 1937)

Vernon Kinietz, "European Civilization as a Determinant of Native American Customs," *American Anthropologist* 42 (1940): 116–21

Herbert C. Kraft, "An Archaeological Overview of the Lower Hudson Valley," in *Many Trails: Indians of the Lower Hudson Valley,* ed. Catherine Coleman Brawer (Katonah, N.Y., 1983), 10–15

Kraft, *The Lenape: Archaeology, History, and Ethnography* (Newark, 1986)

Kraft, "The Northern Lenape in Prehistoric and Early Colonial Times," in *The Lenape Indian: A Symposium,* 1–10

Peter Lindestrom, *Geographia Americae, with an Account of the Delaware Indians Based on Surveys and Notes Made in 1654–1655* (Philadelphia, 1925)

George Henry Loskiel, *History of the Mission of the United Brethren Among the Indians in North America* (London, 1794), vol. 1

John M'Cullough, "A Narrative of the Captivity of John M'Cullough," in *Selections of Some of the Most Interesting Narratives of Outrages Committed By the Indians,* ed. Archibald Loudoun (Carlisle, Pa., 1808–11), 1:252–301

William Newcombe, Jr., "The Culture and Acculturation of the Delaware Indians," *Anthropological Papers: Museum of Anthropology, University of Michigan* 10 (1956): 1–141

Francis Daniel Pastorius, "Circumstantial Geographical Description of Pennsylvania," in *Narratives of Early Pennsylvania,* 353–448

William Penn, "Letter to the Free Society of Traders," in *William Penn and the Founding of Pennsylvania, 1680–1684,* ed. Jean R. Soderlund et al. (Philadelphia, 1983)

Edward Hunter Ross, *Indians of the Passaic Valley* (Newark, 1963)

Henry Rowe Schoolcraft, *Archives of Aboriginal Knowledge* (Washington, D.C., 1860), vol. 6

Frank Speck, *Naskapi: Savage Hunters of the Labrador Peninsula* (Norman, Okla., 1935)

Speck, *A Study of the Delaware Indian Big House Ceremony* (Harrisburg, Pa., 1931)

Frank Speck and Jesse Moses, "The Celestial Bear Comes Down to Earth," *Scientific Publications of the Reading Public Museum and Art Gallery* 7 (1945), 31–32

Robert F. Spencer et al., *The Native Americans: Ethnology and Backgrounds of the North American Indians* (New York, 1977)

Melburn D. Thurman, "Delaware Social Organization," in *A Delaware Indian Symposium,* 111–34

Allen W. Trelease, *Indian Affairs in Colonial New York: The Seventeenth Century* (Ithaca, N.Y., 1960)

Douglas H. Ubelaker, "The Sources and Methodology for Mooney's Estimates of North American Indian Population," in *The Native Population of the Americas in 1492,* ed. William M. Denevan (Madison, Wis., 1976), 243–88

Ruth Underhill, *Red Man's Religion: Belief and Practice of the Indians North of Mexico* (Chicago, 1965)

Adriaen Van der Donck, *A Description of the New Netherlands* (Syracuse, 1968)

Anthony F. C. Wallace, "New Religions Among the Delaware Indians, 1600–1900," *Southwestern Journal of Anthropology* 12 (1956), 1–21

Paul Wallace, *Indians in Pennsylvania,* 2nd ed., rev. William A. Hunter (Harrisburg, Pa., 1981)

Nicholaes Van Wassenaer, "Description and First Settlement of New Netherlands, from Wassenaer's History Van Europa," in *Documentary History of the State of New York,* ed. E. B. O'Callaghan, 4 vols. (Albany, 1850), 3:27–48

Chief Waubuno, *The Traditions of the Delawares, as Told To Chief Waubuno* (London, 1875)

Roger Williams, *A Key Into the Language of America,* ed. John J. Teunissen and Evelyn J. Hinz (Detroit, 1973)

Charles Wolley, *A Two Years' Journal in New York (1701),* ed. Edward G. Bourne (Cleveland, 1902)

Lawrence C. Wroth, ed., *The Voyages of Giovanni da Verrazzano, 1524–1528* (New Haven, 1970)

David Zeisberger, "History of the North American Indians," in *Ohio Archaeological and Historical Society Publications* 19 (1910), 1–189

Chapter Two

Alfred W. Crosby, Jr., *The Columbian Exchange: Biological and Cultural Consequences of 1492* (Westport, Conn., 1972)

Daniel Denton, *A Brief Description of New York (1670)* (Cleveland, 1902)

Daniel Pietersz de Vries, "From the 'Korte Historiael Ende Journals Aenteyckeninge (1655)'," in *Narratives of New Netherland*, 186–234; "Extracts from a Work Called Breeden Raedt," in *Documentary History of the State of New York*, 4:99–112

Robert Steven Grumet, "Children of Muhheahkkunnuck: A Lower River Indian History," in *Many Trails*, 17–24

Robert Steven Grumet, "A New Ethnohistorical Model for North American Indian Demography," *North American Archaeologist* 11 (1990): 29–41

Francis Jennings, *The Ambiguous Iroquois Empire* (New York, 1984)

Amandus Johnson, *The Swedish Settlements on the Delaware* (Philadelphia, 1911), vol. 1

Robert Juet, *Juet's Journal: The Voyage of the Half Moon from 4 April to 7 November 1609*, ed. Robert M. Lunny (Newark, 1959)

Isaac de Rasieres, "Letter from Isaack de Rasieres to the Directors of the Amsterdam Chamber of the West Indian Company," in *Documents Relating to New Netherland, 1624–1626, in the Henry E. Huntington Library and Art Gallery*, trans. A. J. F. Van Laer (San Marino, Calif., 1924), 171–251

Reginald McMahon, "The Achter Col Colony on the Hackensack," *New Jersey History* 89 (1971): 221–40

"Memorial of the Eight Men at Manhattans to the States General, 1643," "Report of the Board of Accounts on New Netherland (1644)," "Information Respecting Land in New Netherland (1650)," and "Report of the Honorable Peter Stuyvesant, Late Director-General ... (1665)" in *Documents Relative to the Colonial History of the State of New York*, ed. E. B. O'Callaghan and Berthold Fernow, 15 vols. (Albany, 1850), 1:139–40, 149–56, 365–71, 2:363–76

Samuel Eliot Morison, *The European Discovery of America: The Northern Voyages, A.D. 500–1600* (New York, 1971)

E. B. O'Callaghan, ed., *Documents Relative to the Colonial History of the State of New York* (Albany, 1856), vol. 1

"Report of Governor Johan Printz, 1664," and "Report of Governor Johan Rising, 1665," in *Narratives of Early Pennsylvania*, 102–04, 156–57

E. M. Ruttenber, *History of the Indian Tribes of Hudson's River* (Albany, 1872)

Gabriel Thomas, "An Historical and Geographical Account of Pennsylvania and of West-New-Jersey," in *Narratives of Early Pennsylvania*, 307–52

C. A. Weslager, *The Delaware Indians, A History* (New Brunswick, 1972)

Thomas Yong, "Relation of Captain Thomas Yong, 1634," in *Narratives of Early Pennsylvania*, 31–49

In addition to these works cited previously: Brasser, "Early Indian-European Contacts"; de Vries, "From the 'Korte Historiael'," in *Narratives of Early Pennsylvania;* Kalm, *Travels in North America;* Lindestrom, *Geographia Americae;* Newcombe, "Culture and Acculturation"; Trelease, *Indian Affairs in Colonial New York;* Van der Donck, *Description of New Netherland;* and Wroth, *Voyages of Giovanni de Verranzano*

Chapter Three

John Bodner, *The Transplanted: A History of Immigrants in Urban America* (Bloomington, Ind., 1985)

Thomas Brainerd, ed., *The Life of John Brainerd, the Brother of David Brainerd, and His Successor as Missionary to the Indians of New Jersey* (Philadelphia and New York, 1874); Bureau of the Census, *Historical Statistics of the United States, Colonial Times to 1970* (Washington, D.C., 1975)

W. E. B. DuBois, *The Souls of Black Folk* (New York, 1969)

Elma Gray, *Wilderness Christians: The Moravian Mission to the Delaware Indians* (1956; reprint, New York, 1973)

Grumet, "We Are Not So Great Fools: Changes in Upper Delawarian Socio-Political Life, 1630–1758," Ph.D. diss. Rutgers University, 1979

Samuel Hazard, *Annals of Pennsylvania from the Discovery of the Delaware, 1609–1682* (Philadelphia, 1850)

Philip E. Howard, Jr., ed. *The Life and Diary of David Brainerd, Edited by Jonathan Edwards* (Chicago, 1949)

Edward M. Larrabee, "Recurrent Themes and Sequences in North American Indian-European Culture Contact," in *Transactions of the American Philosophical Society*, n.s., 66 (1976), 1–48

August Meier, *Negro Thought in America, 1880–1915: Racial Ideology in the Age of Booker T. Washington* (Ann Arbor, Mich., 1963)

Kelly Miller, *Radicals and Conservatives and Other Essays on the Negro in America* (New York, 1968)

John E. Pomfret, *The Province of West New Jersey 1609–1701* (Princeton, 1956)

James "Lone Bear" Revey, "The Delaware Indians in New Jersey, from Colonial Times to the Present," in *The Lenape Indian*, 72–82

"State of the Facts about the Riots from September 19th, 1745, to December 8th, 1746," "Letter from Governor Bernard to the Lords of Trade—(October 31, 1758)," and "Letter from Governor Bernard to the Lords of Trade—(June 15, 1759)" in *Archives of the State*

of New Jersey, ed. William A. Whitehead et al., 1st ser., 30 vols. (Trenton 1880–93), 6:397–418, 9:139–42, 174–76
And these sources cited earlier: Goddard, "Delaware;" Jennings, *Ambiguous Iroquois Empire;* Kalm, *Travels in North America;* Pastorius, "Circumstantial Geographical Description of Pennsylvania"; Trelease, *Indian Affairs in Colonial New York;* Weslager, *The Delaware Indians;* and Wolley, *A Two Years' Journal in New York*

Chapter Four

Bureau of the Census, *Indian Population in the United States and Alaska, 1910* (reprint; New York, 1973) and *1980 Census of Population and Housing, Supplementary Report, Part 32: New Jersey* (Washington, D.C., 1983)
Randolph C. Downes, *Council Fires on the Upper Ohio* (Pittsburgh, 1940)
R. David Edmunds, *The Shawnee Prophet* (Lincoln, Nebr., 1983)
Frank J. Esposito, "The Andarko Delaware of Oklahoma Today," in *The Lenape Indian,* 59–62
William Nelson, *The Indians of New Jersey* (Paterson, 1894)
New Jersey State Data Center, *1980 Census of Population and Housing: Municipal Profiles* (Trenton, 1982), vol. 1
Linda Poolaw, "The Modern Delaware of Western Oklahoma," in *The Lenape Indian,* 58
Terry J. Prewitt, "The Delaware Big House: A Social and Cultural Perception," in *The Lenape Indian,* 50–57
Wiley Sword, *President Washington's Indian War* (Norman, Okla., 1985)
A. Hyatte Verril, *The Real Americans* (New York, 1954)
C. A. Weslager, *The Delaware Westward Migration* (Wallingford, Pa., 1978)
Weslager, "The Munsee, Mahican, and Unami-Delawares," in *Many Trails,* 26–30
In addition to these sources cited earlier: Brainerd, *Life of John Brainerd;* Gray, *Wilderness Christians;* Kraft, *The Lenape: Archaeology, History and Ethnography;* Revey, "The Delaware Indians in New Jersey"; Ubelaker, "Sources and Methodology for Mooney's Estimates"; Weslager, *The Delaware Indians;* and Wroth, *Voyages of Giovanni da Verrazano*

Conclusion

Gary Kriss, "Indians Return to a Spiritual Home," *New York Times, Westchester Weekly,* 22 May 1983

APPENDIX

Sir Edmund Andros (1637–1714). Andros, an English soldier, had a long career of royal service. He was appointed colonial governor of New York in 1674. He assumed that his commission also applied to New Jersey, but this assumption led to continual strife, and in 1681 he was recalled. In 1686, King James II, intent on formulating a comprehensive colonial policy and making the borders of New York and New England defensible, combined the New England colonies into one royal province, the Dominion of New England, and appointed Andros governor. Again Andros alienated the populace and brought on revolt. The Dominion collapsed when news reached America that James II had fled and been replaced by William of Orange. Andros later served as governor of Virginia.

Nora Thompson Dean (d. 1986). One of the last Lenapes to speak the Unami dialect fluently, Dean, also known as "Touching Leaves Woman," generously shared her wide knowledge of Lenape culture with anthropologists, historians, and interested lay persons. From Oklahoma she corresponded actively with scholars, published her own works, and traveled east to conferences in the homeland of her ancestors.

Henry Hudson (?–c. 1611). Hudson, an English navigator, explored part of the North American coast while searching for the northwest passage in 1609. He sailed his ship, the Half Moon, up what was later named the Hudson River to the site of modern-day Albany. On a later voyage, to the bay that was subsequently named after him, he was set adrift by a mutinous crew.

John Killbuck, Jr. (d. 1811). A Lenape whose Indian name was Gelelemend. He became a leading spokesman for those Delawares who wished to remain at peace with the United States during the American Revolution. By 1781 he had lost the support of his people. He fled to Pittsburgh, where he remained until 1785. He died in a mission town in 1811.

Living Solid Face. The Lenapes held that this spirit, also known as *Mesingw,* watched over the deer. To provide themselves with venison

and deerskins, they performed ceremonies dedicated to the Living
Solid Face. In these rituals a dancing figure wearing a mask and a
suit of bearskin appeared as a manifestation of the spirit.

Neolin (fl. 1760–65). Also known as the Delaware Prophet, Neolin lived
among the Lenapes and Shawnees of the Upper Ohio River Country.
He became a religious leader of Pontiac's War, in which several tribes
joined to defend themselves against the British. Neolin urged the
Indians to abandon some European practices, such as the consumption
of alcohol, immediately and to give up others, such as the use of
firearms, gradually. He supported the war against the British because
he believed that the Indians and the British had been created separately and were meant to find spiritual salvation by differing paths.

Richard Nicolls (1624–1672). Nicolls, the first English governor of New
York (1664–68), also served as the governor of New Jersey to 1665.
In 1664, after Charles II seized the colony of New Netherland and
conferred the land on his brother James, Duke of York, Nicolls was
appointed governor of the region. He secured the bloodless surrender
of the Dutch colony and oversaw its transition to English rule.

William Penn (1664–1718). Penn, the English Quaker who founded
Pennsylvania, was also a West Jersey proprietor. In 1681, he received
a Crown grant to territories in North America and established the
Quaker colony of Pennsylvania, named after his father, an English
admiral. He issued a series of liberal charters for Pennsylvania; the
colony was known for friendly relations with the Indians, complete
religious toleration, and an unusually fair criminal code.

Pontiac's War (1763–1765). The Ottawa chief Pontiac, whose name
this war commonly bears, was actually only one of its many leaders.
Another was an important Lenape, Neolin, the Delaware Prophet. The
war was an intertribal effort to drive the British out of the vast region
that stretches from what is now western Pennsylvania and New York
to the Mississippi River. The war ended in something of a stalemate.
On the one hand, the Indians forced the British to abandon nine forts
and to promise not to settle west of the crest of the Appalachians.
The British, on the other hand, continued to maintain a strong
presence. They retained the important forts of Pittsburgh, Niagara, and
Detroit, reestablished others, and replaced the French garrisons in the
Illinois country.

Arthur St. Clair (1736–1818). A brigadier general in the Continental
Line during the American Revolution, St. Clair served as governor
of the Northwest Territory (much of what is now the Midwest) between
1787 and 1802. In 1791 he marched against the Indians, but his army
was defeated by a smaller force from many tribes under the leadership

of the brilliant Miami chief, Little Turtle. This defeat stands as the worst loss ever suffered by a United States Army in a battle with Indians.

Henry Rowe Schoolcraft (1793–1864). Geologist, explorer, Indian agent and early anthropologist, Schoolcraft married an Indian woman. He collected information and wrote extensively about Indian culture. His *Historical and Statistical Information Respecting the History, Condition, and Prospects of the Indian Tribes of the United States,* published in 1851, is still a valuable source.

The Shawnee Prophet (1775?–1834?). Known as Tenskwatawa, the Shawnee Prophet advised his followers to avoid liquor, to refuse to sell land to the United States, and to return to the ways of their ancestors as far as possible. His brother was the war leader Tecumseh. Between 1805 and 1811 the Prophet had a great following, but after his main village was attacked and dispersed by William Henry Harrison at the Battle of Tippecanoe (1811) he lost much prestige. He continued to live among the Shawnees as they, like the Lenapes, migrated westward. He died in Kansas.

Frank Gouldsmith Speck (1881–1950). A University of Pennsylvania anthropologist of Dutch and American Indian background, Speck wrote extensively on Native American language, religion, and culture. Speck and the Indians who made his work possible had enormous respect for each other. During his final days, six separate Native American communities held healing ceremonies in efforts to restore his failing health.

Moses Tunda Tatamy (c. 1695–c. 1760). Tatamy, a convert to Presbyterianism, was among the most prominent New Jersey Indians during the imperial wars of the mid-eighteenth century. He served as an interpreter in several negotiations between British colonists and Lenapes from New Jersey and Pennsylvania. He was an important figure in the arrangements that established the Indian community of Brotherton.

Tecumseh (1768–1813). Tecumseh, the brother of the Shawnee Prophet, was the most famous leader of a movement to unite all the Indians from the northern Great Lakes to the Gulf of Mexico in defense of their lands. The movement suffered a serious blow at the Battle of Tippecanoe (1811) and dissolved during the War of 1812. Tecumseh was killed at the battle of Thames, Ontario, in 1813.

Giovanni da Verrazano (1485?–1528). This Florentine navigator discovered New York and Narragansett bays while exploring the coast of North America in 1524.

Anthony Wayne (1745–1796). This Revolutionary war general was nicknamed "Mad Anthony," apparently because of a rash temper. However, he proved the name wrong in his thoughtful generalship. He led a methodical expedition against the Indians of the Great Lakes and Ohio Valley region and won a decisive victory at the Battle of Fallen Timbers (1794). The Lenape Indians gave up most of their Ohio lands in the treaty that Wayne negotiated at Greenville, Ohio (1795).

White Eyes (d. 1778). An influential Lenape leader and diplomat during the period when the Lenapes lived in the upper Ohio Valley and became known as the Delaware Indians. White Eyes encouraged his people to maintain good relations with the colonies and later with the United States. He died in 1778. At the time it was reported that he had died of smallpox, but the American Indian agent George Morgan later stated that American settlers had murdered him.

SOURCES: *Dictionary of American Biography* 20 vol. and supplements (New York: 1928–37, 1944–81); William A. Hunter, "Moses Tunda Tatamy, Delaware Indian Diplomat," in *A Delaware Indian Symposium* ed., Herbert C. Kraft (Harrisburg, 1974); Herbert C. Kraft, *The Lenape: Archaeology, History, and Ethnography* (Newark, 1986).

SUGGESTIONS FOR FURTHER READING

Brawer, Catherine Coleman. *Many Trails: Indians of the Lower Hudson Valley.* Katonah, New York: The Katonah Gallery, 1983. This collection of fine essays includes photographs both of items from the Lenape archaeological record and of living Lenapes.

Cross, Dorothy. *New Jersey's Indians: Report No. 1, New Jersey State Museum.* Trenton: New Jersey State Museum, 1965. This clearly written volume emphasizes the material aspects of Lenape life, and briefly discusses Lenape thought and history. Illustrations. Bibliography.

Harrington, Mark R. *Dickon Among the Indians.* Chicago, Philadelphia: John C. Winston, 1938. Reissued as *The Indians of New Jersey, Dickon Among the Lenapes.* New Brunswick: Rutgers University Press, 1963. In this novel by a noted anthropologist, a shipwrecked English boy is taken in by the Lenapes. First enslaved and later adopted, the boy learns both women's and men's work. More recent scholarship casts doubt upon many of Harrington's assumptions about traditional Lenape culture, particularly the presence of servitude, but the work nonetheless reveals the Lenape world view with great sensitivity. Illustrations.

————. *Religion and Ceremonies of the Lenape.* Indian Notes and Monographs, vol. 3. New York: Museum of the American Indian, Heye Foundation, 1921. This scholarly work combines twentieth-century fieldwork among the Western Lenapes with references to early historical sources. Illustrations. Bibliography. Index.

Jennings, Francis, *The Ambiguous Iroquois Empire: The Covenant Chain Confederation of Indian Tribes with English Colonies from its beginnings to the Lancaster Treaty of 1744.* New York: W. S. Norton, 1984. This scholarly work reveals the complexity of relations among the Six Nations, the English, the Lenapes, and other peoples. Maps. Bibliography. Index.

Kraft, Herbert C. *The Lenape: Archaeology, History, and Ethnography,* Newark: New Jersey Historical Society, 1986. Written for the general public by the foremost scholar of New Jersey Indians, this volume offers a particularly rich synthesis of New Jersey archaeology.

_____, ed. *A Delaware Indian Symposium.* Harrisburg: Pennsylvania Historical and Museum Commission, 1974. A collection of essays by archaeologists, historians, linguists, and anthropologists. Maps. Illustrations. Bibliographies.

_____, ed. *The Lenape Indian: A Symposium.* South Orange, N.J.: Seton Hall University, 1984. In addition to essays by professional archaeologists, historians, and anthropologists, this volume includes valuable essays by Lenapes.

Larrabee, Edward M. *Recurrent Themes and Sequences in North American Indian-European Culture Contact.* Transactions of the American Philosophical Society. n.s., 66: 1976. This investigation of broad patterns in the history of American Indian reservations chooses Brotherton as a case study. Maps. Charts. Illustrations. Bibliography. Index.

Newcombe, William Jr. *The Culture and Acculturation of the Delaware Indians.* Anthropological Papers, Museum of Anthropology, University of Michigan. 10 (1956): 1–141. This scholarly work describes changes in Lenape culture following European contact. Fascinating Lenape myths are also discussed. Charts. Bibliography.

Spencer, Robert F., and Jennings, Jesse D., *et al. The Native Americans: Ethnology and Backgrounds of the North American Indians.* New York: Harper and Row, 1977. This is the standard text on North American Indian cultures. Rich in detail, it is unfortunately encumbered by scientific prose. Illustrations. Maps. Bibliography, Index.

Trelease, Allen W., *Indian Affairs in Colonial New York: The Seventeenth Century.* Ithaca: Cornell University Press, 1960. This thoroughly researched piece of scholarship focuses mainly on the Iroquois, but for the history of New Jersey's Indians north of the Raritan River, this is the place to start. Maps. Illustrations. Bibliography. Index.

Trigger, Bruce, ed. *Handbook of North American Indians,* vol. 15: *Northeast.* Washington, D.C.: Smithsonian Institution, 1978. A critical reference work, with several articles by leading scholars that relate to Lenape history and culture. Maps. Bibliography. Illustrations. Index.

Van der Donck, Adraien. *A Description of the New Netherland (1656).* Syracuse: Syracuse University Press, 1968. The only primary source included in this bibliography, this evocative work describes Lenape culture.

Wallace, Anthony F. C. *King of the Delawares: Teedyuscung, 1700–1763.* Philadelphia: University of Pennsylvania Press, 1949. This beautifully written biography of a Susquehanna River Lenape (born in New Jersey), is also a history of the western Lenapes in the eighteenth century. Maps. Bibliographical footnotes. Index.

Wallace, Paul. *Indians in Pennsylvania.* 2d ed., rev. William A. Hunter. Harrisburg: Pennsylvania Historical and Museum Commission, 1981 (1st ed., 1961). Written by a scholar for the general public, the work conveys Lenape history and culture in a sympathetic and highly readable manner. Maps. Illustrations. Bibliographical footnotes. Index.

Weslager, Clinton Alfred. *The Delaware Indians, a History.* New Brunswick: Rutgers University Press, 1972. A scholarly work aimed at a popular audience, this is undoubtedly the basic work on the Lenapes. For New Jersey history, the work is especially strong in its discussion of Lenapes who lived both south of the Raritan River and in the Delaware Valley. Illustrations. Maps. Bibliographical footnotes. Index.

_____ . *The Delaware Westward Migration.* Wallingford, Pennsylvania: Middle Atlantic Press, 1978. A discussion of the Lenapes' trials as they took many paths to the West. Illustrations. Maps. Index. Documents.

_____ . *The Delawares: A Critical Bibliography.* Bloomington: Indiana University Press, 1978. With this entry, we end where any further study should begin. Though Weslager's bibliography is a decade old, it is still authoritative.